"*Following Jesus* is especially needed at this time as Friends consider how to minister authentically to a new people to be gathered. I am convinced it will play an important role in the current renewal of the Friends message. All Quakers—evangelical, moderate, pastoral, progressive, unprogrammed—should spend time with this important and powerful book."

J. Brent Bill
author of *Sacred Compass* and other books

"Paul Anderson has given the Friends church a tool that serves many purposes. It can be used to introduce someone to Christian faith or to deepen the faith and practice of someone who has been a lifelong follower of Christ. It can be used for group study and reflection or for personal growth. All who read this will find it applies to them just as they are."

Jamie Johnson
director of the Friends Leadership Program, George Fox University

"The crucial issue of life for a Christian is following Jesus. Nothing is more important, or more challenging, and Paul Anderson shows us the way. Here is a book that is soundly biblical, intellectually stimulating, and personally impelling. This book will change your life, renew your commitment, and could revive your church."

Lloyd John Ogilvie
president of Leadership Unlimited;
former Chaplain of the United States Senate

"Paul's book is a wonderful blend of good biblical scholarship, Quaker history, and spiritual formation. More than that, it gets to the heart of the Quaker vision, which is an invitation to walk faithfully in the way of Jesus. As a Friends pastor, I am grateful for this book that speaks to our condition at a time when we need it most."

Scott Wagoner
pastor, Deep River Friends Meeting

"Here is a practical resource to guide Christians of our generation in a contagious, life-transforming journey of following Jesus. Writing from the perspective of an evangelical Friend, Paul Anderson combines his own brilliant teaching on Jesus' timeless truths with the counsel of Christian spiritual leaders throughout church history."

David Kingrey
chair of the Division of Bible/Theology, Barclay College

"*Following Jesus* is a wonderful book for rejuvenating the essence of Quaker spirituality, describing a living relationship which encounters Jesus every day. This involves meeting Jesus personally and working in the gifts of the Spirit, and results in changed lives."

Eric William Middleton
former principal, Prior Pursglove College (Guisborough, UK);
author of *Dimensions of the Spirit*

"Paul Anderson, an internationally respected biblical scholar, has written faithfully over the years, calling Friends to increased understanding and faithfulness. It is a joy to see these writings in one helpful volume. Open to any page and you will be illumined, challenged, and inspired."

Jan Wood
director, Good News Associates

"Paul Anderson provides a welcome and valued link between our evangelical call to actively and intentionally live our life in Christ and our desire to do so in ways that reflect our Quaker testimonies. His treatment of 'convincement versus coercion' alone is worth the read."

David A. King
president, Malone University

"In this beautifully organized survey of Christian discipleship, Paul Anderson succeeds in showing us, with urgency and humor—and zero parochial narrowness—just what he means when he says, 'The more I learn about the New Testament, the more Quaker I become.'"

Johan Maurer
clerk, Moscow Friends Meeting (Russia);
former pastor, Reedwood Friends Church

"Paul Anderson has produced a deeply spiritual message about the heart of Quaker Christianity. He persuades us to live as Friends of Jesus, committed to a humble and universal ministry, whose 'testimonies'—not denominational 'distinctives'—are shown in everyday actions."

Hugh Barbour
emeritus professor of Quaker history, Earlham College

"Far more than an overview of Quaker testimonies, *Following Jesus* is a clearly written introduction to those beliefs that stand at the very core of the Christian faith. It is hard to imagine a follower of Jesus who would not be edified—and challenged—by the plain truths this book proclaims."

Bill Jolliff
professor of English, George Fox University

"Anderson's *Following Jesus* is an astonishing gift to our current conversation in religion. Part *apologia* and part exposition of positions that characterize Quaker theology and praxis, *Following Jesus* is an insider's look into a stream of Christianity that is of expanding importance to anyone who hopes to understand twenty-first century latinized Christianity — where it's coming from, and what it has been informed by."

Phyllis Tickle
author of *The Great Emergence* and *Emergence Christianity*

"Paul Anderson's love for the Friends community resounds throughout this work. Though a scholar by trade, Paul's pastoral heart and concern emerges as he urges those of us in the Quaker community to move beyond thinking and talking about our faith — to actually practicing it in the ordinary and extra-ordinary life we share in Christ."

Colin Saxton
general secretary, Friends United Meeting

"Sincerity is the hallmark of the Quaker approach to Christianity presented by Paul Anderson, and it shines from every page. In a series of approachable yet well-considered discussions, readers are challenged to consider how they can best fulfill their vocation to minister to others. The rich resources of the Quaker tradition and the encouragement they offer to a life of ministry are set out with clarity and compassion."

Hugh Pyper
professor of biblical interpretation, University of Sheffield

"Anderson's collection of essays is elegantly written, lavishly sourced, deftly argued, and as convincing as they are convicting."

Leonard Sweet
best-selling author; E. Stanley Jones Professor, Drew University;
distinguished visiting professor, George Fox University

"Paul Anderson has produced for all followers of Jesus an excellent review of what life in Christ is about and how it should be practically lived. He includes what many biblical scholars ignore, namely our experience with the risen Christ. While some Christians may have questions about his view of sacramentalism, Anderson makes an important defense of the contribution of Quaker theology to our understanding of the Christian faith. His well-known biblical scholarship is joined here with a gracious and thoughtful discussion of the experience of the life that Christ has called us to live."

Lee Martin McDonald
president emeritus, Acadia Divinity College (Canada)

Following Jesus

The Heart of Faith and Practice

by Paul Anderson

BARCLAY PRESS
Newberg, OR 97132

FOLLOWING JESUS
The Heart of Faith and Practice

© 2013 by Paul Anderson

BARCLAY PRESS
Newberg, OR
www.barclaypress.com
www.barclaypress.com/paulanderson

COVER DESIGN BY DARRYL BROWN

ISBN 978-1-59498-028-2

Contents

Acknowledgments
and Dedication

All of the present essays are either new or modified from earlier published forms — most of the latter appeared in the *Evangelical Friend*, which I edited from 1990 to 1994. These include:

> "On Following Jesus" (1994)
> "The Present Leadership of the Resurrected Lord"
> (1989, also published in *Quaker Life*)
> "The Power of the Good News" (1991)
> "On Being Great Commission Quakers" (1992)
> "Transforming Worship" (1994)
> "Embracing the Silence" (1991, also published
> in *Quaker Life*)
> "Members of the Crew" (1993)
> "The Universal Ministry" (1991)
> "A Theology of Presence" (1993)
> "On the Character of Sacramentality" (1992)
> "On the Sovereignty of Nations and the
> Kingdom of God" (1991).

I am grateful to Dean Gregory, Jack Willcuts, and Lon Fendall for their exemplary editorial service before me, and to Howard Macy, Becky Ankeny, Janelle Olivarez, and Dan McCracken for the privilege of working on the *Evangelical Friend* together.

The best way to reflect is to preach; the best way to learn is to teach. I am greatly indebted to those congregations I have served as a Friends pastor (West River Friends Meeting, Reedwood Friends Church, Clackamas Park Friends Church) and to my students at George Fox University for allowing me to test ideas and also to learn from those I serve. I also appreciate being able to develop some of these themes within the Quaker

Theological Discussion Group, with which I have engaged for more than a couple of decades, and the Christian Forum Class at Reedwood Friends Church, where presentations on several of these themes have been made.

I thank my family for their support and encouragement over the years. My parents, Alvin and Lucy Anderson, have inspired so many in their Christ-centered Quaker faith; it is a high privilege indeed to further their influence in written form. I also am grateful to my wife, Carla, and our three daughters—Sarah, Della, and Olivia—for their support over the years. We've discussed many of these ideas together, and we continue to learn from each other in seeking to know and obey the truth.

Finally, I want to thank Arthur Roberts for his leadership and mentorship; this book is dedicated to Arthur. I am deeply indebted to his life of faithfulness in following Jesus in such powerful and exemplary ways.

"Meister Eckhart wrote: 'There are plenty to follow our Lord half-way, but not the other half. They will give up possessions, friends and honors, but it touches them too closely to disown themselves.' It is just this astonishing life which is willing to follow Him the other half, sincerely to disown itself, this life which intends complete obedience, without any reservations, that I would propose to you in all humility, in all boldness, in all seriousness. I mean this literally, utterly, completely, and I mean it for you and for me—commit your lives in unreserved obedience to Him."[1] **(Thomas Kelly**, 1941)

1. Thomas Kelly, *A Testament of Devotion* (HarperOne, 1996), 26.

Prologue

The Dedicated Life

Is your life given totally, unreservedly, to God? It can be. Further, it deserves to be, as God is the source and ground of our being—the origin and destiny of life itself. Indeed, there can be no authentic religion, no effective spirituality, without a pervasive and ongoing stance of openness and receptivity to the divine presence and will. We were created for this human-divine relationship, and until we open ourselves to this life-changing reality, we fail to experience the full power and meaning of life itself.

But the way is fraught with obstacles. We may fear what we do not know or disdain what we misunderstand. And yet, the loving God revealed in Jesus dissuades our fears, evoking a fitting sense of awe over such a possibility. Or, we may misconstrue or misname this life, regarding it as a recipe for things that "worked" or a map we can follow instead of following the Master. And yet, the living Christ works within us and among us in ways undeniable if we will but attend his gentle promptings.

The dedicated life is no mere religious platform or cluster of doctrinal loyalties. It is fundamentally a *living relationship*; each day the manna from heaven must be freshly gathered up and taken in anew lest it spoil and cease to nourish. Living in a believing responsiveness to the Lord is the singular priority of true followers of Jesus, and now is the time for a renewed or initial commitment to holy attentiveness and holy obedience. As Thomas Kelly invites, *may we commit our lives in unreserved obedience to him.*

Just as the dedicated life is not a religious platform or creed, neither should we regard it as a special calling for some and not the sort of thing common persons should attempt. Quite the opposite! The dedicated life is not just for special temperaments or religious elites. Rather, the life of givenness to God is meant to be the *normal*—the *basic*—Christian life. If all would live it, how different our world would be! In fact, one reason many fail to be impressed by religion today is that so few of its members have lived into the heart of the calling to be *given* children, men, and women. It is the source of all true happiness, but happiness cannot be its goal. Rather, true fulfillment comes only in being poured out as a living offering to God—spilled out in love as a healing balm for the world. It is the life that you and I are truly meant to live, and it only begins as our clinging to *anything* else comes to an end.

The goal of this book is not to comment on the lowest common denominator among Christians; it is to explore our highest common purpose, and to do so with the benefit of the wisdom of a particular tradition that has sought to do so for three-and-a-half centuries. In that sense, I write on radical Christian discipleship proper, but I do so from an evangelical Quaker's perspective. As pilgrims toward the heavenly city help one another along the way, so we learn from others. We illumine the path for one another and encourage each other in the venture. After all, it is a great journey we are on, yet we do not travel alone.

Thomas Kelly goes on to say, "In some, says William James, religion exists as a dull habit, in others as an acute fever. Religion as a dull habit is not that for which Christ lived and died."[2] While the Quaker movement has been a living testimonial to this conviction, God has no grandchildren. Every generation must drink anew from the springs of living water and set its sails to the winds of the Spirit. Despite our

2. Kelly, *A Testament of Devotion* (HarperOne, 1996), 27.

endeavors, though, encountering the Divine is never a given; it is always a matter of responsiveness and trust. The dynamic combination of living faith and faithful praxis forms the solid foundation upon which the dedicated life is grounded. As we explore the adventure together, I thank you for joining me across constraints of time and space. Following the Lord the other half of the way is where all things indeed become *new*!

"Now after I had received that opening from the Lord that
to be bred at Oxford or Cambridge was not sufficient
to fit a man to be a minister of Christ, I regarded
the priests less and looked more after the dissenting
people....As I had forsaken all the priests, so I left
the separate preachers also, and those called the most
experienced people; for I saw there was none among them
all that could speak to my condition. And when all my
hopes in them and in all men were gone, so that I had
nothing outwardly to help me, nor could I tell what to
do, then, oh then, I heard a voice which said, 'There is
one, even Christ Jesus, that can speak to thy condition,'
and when I heard it my heart did leap for joy." **(George Fox,** 1647)

"As I had a time to preach the Truth amongst you, to the
convincement of many, so also now I have a time to seal
the same with patient suffering in the bonds of the gospel,
that you may see that it is no other but what we are made
able and willing to seal with patient suffering, yea, with our
blood, if we be called to it....Be willing that self shall suffer
for the Truth, and not the Truth for self." **(James Parnell,** 1655)

"Christ our leader is worthy of being
followed in his leadings at all times." **(John Woolman,** 1772)

"You are my friends if you do what I command
you. I do not call you servants any longer,
because the servant does not know what the
master is doing; but I have called you friends,
because I have made known to you everything
that I have heard from my Father. You did not
choose me but I chose you. And I appointed you
to go and bear fruit, fruit that will last, so that
the Father will give you whatever you ask him
in my name. I am giving you these commands
so that you may love one another." **(Jesus,** John 15:14-17 NRSV)

Following
Jesus

On Following Jesus

Some Christian groups ask, "How can we be certain of our salvation?" Others wonder, "How can we be sure we are right?" Still others inquire, "How can we do good in the world?" The Quaker question, however, has been, "How can we be—most radically and effectively—true followers of Jesus?" When this question is lived faithfully, the other questions tend to take care of themselves.

Fortunately, Friends are not the only ones to ask what it means to follow Jesus centrally. Other than the Bible, the most popular book of the Middle Ages was Thomas à Kempis's *The Imitation of Christ*, and to this day it remains a devotional classic. Charles Sheldon's book *In His Steps* became one of the most widely read Christian books of the twentieth century, asking, "What would Jesus do?" Not a bad question. And, Richard Foster's *Celebration of Discipline* came to be recognized as a best-selling classic within a decade or two of its writing. Even current interests in Christian discipleship and spirituality center on the question: "How can people today follow Jesus effectively?" Thankfully, Quakers are not alone in asking

An earlier version of "Following Jesus" was first published in *Evangelical Friend* in 1994.

that question; we have a lot to learn from others who also share this quest.

The truth is, though, we also have much to share, and the body of Christ (and the world beyond) will be worse off if Friends neglect proper stewardship of the truth with which we have been entrusted. On this matter, church-growth "experts" have played us false. Churches that grow are not necessarily those that de-emphasize a particular heritage. If this were true, cults would be extinct instead of on the rise. Churches that grow are those that are clear about their priorities, can articulate them well, and embody them meaningfully. May I add one more? Churches that grow healthily are also those where the Spirit of the risen Lord reigns powerfully and transformingly — where people *follow Jesus* enthusiastically and support one another in that common venture. There's no substitute for authentic and contagious spirituality!

At times I hear a comment suggesting evangelical Friends emphasize more pointedly the following of Jesus Christ instead of Quaker "distinctives." If one means by this that we should never mistake the external trappings of a movement (such as quaint expressions, symbolic dress, and external trademarks) for the center, I agree wholeheartedly. But if one holds this perspective while considering Christian testimonies on peace, simplicity, spiritual worship and sacraments, inclusive and empowered ministry, integrity, and evangelism by convincement rather than coercion, that person understands neither the heart of Quakerism nor what it means to follow Jesus. Distinctives are incidental — time-bound expressions of spiritual concerns; testimonies, however, are central — timeless truths of the gospel that every generation needs to express anew. Spiritual revival and social reform go hand in hand; they involve Christian testimonies as the central convictions of faith and practice.

When you set out to follow Jesus completely, wholly, unreservedly, you will be confronted, in time, with every one of the issues Quakers have been addressing over the last three-and-a-half centuries. And these were issues faced squarely by early Christians too. Apostolic Christianity has less to do with calendars or institutions, and more to do with encountering Jesus Christ personally and being sent by him as a partner in his saving, healing, redeeming work. This encountering and partnering makes one a "friend" of Jesus (John 15:14-17). Friends of Jesus have some knowledge of what Jesus is about and seek to obey what he commands.

May an authentic follower of Jesus *ever* lie, cheat, or kill for an earthly or a heavenly cause? Jesus says *no*. In fact, such departures from the way of Christ actually set back the active reign of God. Does pleasing God and developing a meaningful relationship with God *ever* hinge upon performing an external act or saying the right words, separate from an inward response of genuine faith to the divine initiative? To say so makes a mockery of the cross. Jesus came to show us the way to God, and he died to unite humanity with God. In doing so, he revealed with finality the bankruptcy of all human approaches to God; he did not create a new set of Christian forms to replace Jewish ones. If Christ is enough, nothing else is needed. Forms may assist, but they never determine God's saving, healing, empowering action toward us. Forms can also get in the way, eclipsing the directly mediated work of the Lord. If we add *anything* to Christ, we thereby diminish the all-sufficiency of his work.

Is Christ's present will for his disciples ever locked into a set of regulations or system of beliefs? We need to understand what we believe, but doctrine does not save us. The Scriptures teach that the Holy Spirit, the Spirit of Christ, will be present to guide his followers into all truth, convicting them of sin and of righteousness (John 14–16). Belief in the resurrection is one thing; living in the power and presence of the resurrected Lord is another. Such is central to the good news of the gospel.

But how do we do it? Ironically, Friends have traditionally held that we must ever attend to and heed the risen Lord above and beyond human traditions. So, an appeal to "traditional Quakerism" is a contradiction of terms. On the other hand, when we set out to follow Jesus, we are not the first, nor are we alone. Others have found his teachings convincing and his leadings true. To discard the benefit of those learnings is foolishness, although to become smug in them is to deny their central genius. Following Jesus is a dynamic reality, going to the very heart of all aspects of faith and practice. This endeavor forms our convictions and transforms our actions, continuing to call out to us as a lifelong venture.

At different stages of our lives, following Jesus addresses different challenges. As a child it might mean seeking to be kind and patient, living in more generous and less self-centered ways. As an adolescent it might mean living by a Christian ethic instead of giving in to the pressures of the world. These challenges are always with us, of course, but as an adult, we might face not only questions about personal lifestyles, attitudes, and behaviors, but also questions about what kind of world this should be and how Christians ought to make a difference in it for Christ. While the early Christian and the early Quaker movements were essentially energized by the young, the potency of believers in every generation involves being drawn into partnership with Christ, following his lead in redeeming and healing a world beloved of God.

As the Lord speaks to me about following him today, I find my Quaker heritage of more significance, not less. I suppose that not only are we a people who ask what it means to follow Jesus, but in a real sense, we *are* that question. But beware! The true answer might not come in the form of fine-sounding propositions or creeds. As important as these things are, we will find the truest answers in the changed and changing lives of those who encounter Jesus personally and whom Jesus sends as his apostolic partners in the world. These people, regardless of the movement they ascribe to, Jesus calls his friends.

On Reviving Primitive and Apostolic Christianity

Nearly every renewal movement in the history of Christianity has sought to recover at least some particular aspect of the vitality of the early church. In the second century, a movement called the Montanists sought to recover the Spirit-based power of apostolic Christianity, which had become distorted by institutionalization. The Benedictines, the Franciscans, the Carmelites, and many other orders and reform movements within the Catholic Church sought to restore some aspect of pristine Christian faith and practice, as did the Reformers with their return to the authority of Scripture. This, likewise, was the vision of early Friends. They sought not to create a "denomination" of the Christian faith or even to become a movement within it. They sought to recover the basic faith and practice of the apostles — restoring the days of the early church before Christianity became the official religion (seen as "apostasy"), and reviving primitive, apostolic Christianity.

That, of course, was a tall order! Whereas noted hierarchical approaches to apostolic succession have seen the apostolic lineage as a physical one—with one bishop laying hands
on another, tracing the line back to the apostles—Friends saw
apostolic succession as a spiritual reality hinging upon the
outpouring of the Holy Spirit, just as it was for the apostles
and every vital chapter of church history. The Spirit is not limited to geography or tradition; but as the wind blows where it
will, so the Spirit moves unconstrained and unpredicted. The
way Friends approached apostolic vitality, therefore, was to
make encountering and responding to the living Lord the center of faith and practice, seeking to recover the dynamic spiritual life of the apostolic era. William Penn called it "primitive
Christianity revived." Joseph John Gurney thus called the
Quaker movement "the religion of the New Testament our
Lord and Saviour Jesus Christ, without diminution, without
addition, and without compromise."[3] It was called by some
"Christianity writ plain." Elton Trueblood called it "Basic
Christianity."

These aspirations might seem a bit overstated to us
today, and they probably were even back then. As Robert
Hess, professor of philosophy at Malone University, used to
say, "The past isn't what it used to be..., and perhaps it
never was." When you read the Bible closely, it becomes all
too clear that the early church never was a perfect community,
nor is it ever possible for later movements to recover the
identical semblance of earlier ones. Many parallels, however,
did emerge as early Friends sought to recover the vitality
of the pristine movement of Jesus and his followers. For
instance, like the first Christians, early Friends sought to

---

3. Joseph John Gurney, *Impartiality in the Interpretation of Scripture*
(New York: Isaac Hopper, 1841), 16.

embody the character of New Testament Christianity in the following ways:

- They emphasized the essence of spiritual vitality rather than fixating upon outward religious measures or patterns.

- They proclaimed the good news of the gospel to all who would listen, locally and around the world, seeking to carry forth the Great Commission of Jesus into all nations.

- They sought to live by the power and present leading of the risen Christ, individually and corporately, declaring that Christ is indeed present to teach his people himself.

- They believed God was no respecter of persons, and that before God all are equal, including women, men, children, and persons of varying social statuses, races, and backgrounds.

- They saw others as being created in the image of God and worked to improve the conditions of the disenfranchised in the name of Jesus' love.

- They emphasized worship in Spirit and in truth, with authenticity transcending forms and locations, seeking to abide in that place inhabited by the prophets out of which they wrote the Scriptures.

- They sought to live with absolute integrity, loving others with the transforming love of Christ, letting their *yes* be yes and their *no* be no.

- They experienced outpourings of the Holy Spirit and divine visitations in ways reminiscent of rushing winds and tongues of fire at that first Christian Pentecost.

- They were led to speak prophetically to the needs of the world and were given gifts of healing and faith, by which the world began to change.

- They called for putting away the sword, as Jesus commanded his followers, and they spoke truth to those in power as required of them spiritually.

- They embraced the ideals of Christ's kingdom rather than settling for givens in the world; as a young person's movement, they called for religion and society alike to change in response to God's dynamic leadership in the world.

In these and other ways, early Friends sought to recover the essence of the apostolic Jesus movement. Water is always purest near the headwaters of the spring, and early Friends saw themselves fulfilling the Bible's teachings on how the Spirit of the risen Christ not only led the church back then, but also how Christ seeks to lead the church today. In contrast to the staid religion of their day, and over against the yoking of religious power to political agendas, early Friends saw the essence of Christianity as involving life-changing encounters with the Divine. In that sense, they sought to play the role of partners with Christ in furthering his saving, healing, redeeming mission in the world, and such is the calling of authentic believers today.

So, how did early Friends do in that restorationist venture? The movement grew to more than 50,000 within its first 50 years, and when these early Friends migrated to America, Penn's woods (Pennsylvania) became a destination for persecuted Christians from all over Europe, especially those suffering (oddly enough) for refusing to support magistrates and their military ventures. Indeed, Quaker convictions regarding liberty of conscience and equal access to God's truth influenced the spirit of American democratic ideals as much as any other movement. Friends, therefore, influenced the history of the larger world far more than their modest numbers suggest.

Additionally, many other spiritual movements have their own roots in the Quaker awakening. The Wesleyan Methodist movement, the Pentecostal movement, the Salvation Army, the Vineyard Fellowship—the Quaker desire to follow Jesus radically and to restore Christianity to its pristine and apostolic character directly influenced all of these movements. The greatest measure of the impact of the Friends movement might not be a simple counting of its 400,000 members around the world today, but consideration of its larger and more generous impact. The number of charismatic Christians around the world currently totals nearly half a billion, and many of these are *within* established churches. The contagious impact of post-Azusa Street Spirit-based Christianity since 1906 might well be considered the greatest religious phenomenon in recent world history. Likewise, peace work and social concern by Christians and others have been one of the most significant moral movements in the world within the last century. Of course, Friends cannot claim full credit for either of these developments, but they have been directly involved, and in both cases Friendly contributions have been substantive, even if not credited with a byline. Celebrating the advance of Christ's kingdom above one's own success, perceived or real, is the essence of kingdom living.

It is a mistake, however, to assume that we can find any measure of success in assessing the outcomes of discipleship. Jesus calls us not to be successes but to be faithful, and the true measure of authentic discipleship is always one of faithfulness. Given the example and clear teachings of Jesus, and given his ongoing work through the Holy Spirit, the central Christian question is not simply "What *would* Jesus do?" but also "What *is* Jesus *doing*—in the church and in the world?" Therefore, in seeking to revive primitive and apostolic Christianity, our focus becomes less a matter of imitating an outward pattern and more a focus upon how true followers of Jesus might live in such proximity to the life-giving Word of God that the work of the apostles can continue in this and every generation. When we live out this new focus, imitation of a movement gives way to a far more important reality—

responsiveness to the risen Lord. And, when that happens, primitive Christianity is indeed revived, and apostolic succession is effectively actualized.

One Body, Many Parts

Attempts to understand the ethos and calling of the Quaker movement have been many. In 1966 Lewis Benson wrote a book on *Catholic Quakerism*, in which he laid out the universal Friendly vision for all of Christianity. Hugh Barbour responded with an essay entitled "Protestant Quakerism," in which he located the Friendly vocation within the biblical wing of the Radical Reformation.[4] In a real sense, both are right. As a movement, Friends have both sought to recover "Basic Christianity," connecting the vitality of primitive Christianity with the pressing needs of the world.[5] And yet, the movement is a relatively modest one, and like every other Christian group, is not the whole but merely a part of the larger body of Christ. That being the case, however, how do we live into the role and charge of this particular group within the larger Christian movement? How do we learn from and contribute to other followers of Jesus as we seek to reach the beloved world for whom Christ died?

On the one hand, Friends and every group must de-emphasize and release a particular history and place within the larger movement. Over half a century ago, Elton Trueblood declared that we live now in the "post-denominational era." Not only was that statement correct, as Christians have

---

4. Lewis Benson, *Catholic Quakerism* (Gloucester, UK: Lewis Benson, 1966); Hugh Barbour, "Protestant Quakerism," *Quaker Religious Thought* #22 (1969).

5. See D. Elton Trueblood's collection of essays on Quakerism, *Basic Christianity*, ed. James Newby (Richmond, IN: Friends United Press, 1978).

more and more cooperated across lines of membership and traditional loyalties to work together for Christ and the furthering of his work in the world, it was also *true*. The day is past—and should be—for Christians to remain provincial and sectarian in an age, when the world needs desperately to be reached by the saving and redeeming work of Christ. The question is how to do so, individually and collectively

We are thus called to be followers of the One who is the way, the truth, and the life (John 14:6), and what is done for him and the truth will alone stand at the end of time. In that sense, to seek and find truth is to seek and find Christ; and, to draw closer to Christ is to approximate the truth. It is therefore liberating truth around which all religious ventures and spiritual realities orbit, not the other way around. Whereas all other religions of the world aspire to learn from the experience and teachings of their founders, the heart of vital Christianity involves seeking not simply to imitate its founder, but to encounter and follow the *Founder*. As Samuel Taylor Coleridge put it trenchantly:

> He who begins by loving Christianity better than Truth will proceed by loving his own sect or church better than Christianity, and end by loving himself better than all.[6]

Christ therefore invites us to embrace his yoke—one that fits properly and with which the burdens of life can be borne, as his yoke is easy and his burden is light (Matthew 11:28-30). He also invites us to learn "of" him, but the word in Greek can also mean learning "from" him. In the Gospel of John, Jesus promises to lead his followers into all truth by means of

---

6. Cited from *Aids to Reflection: Moral and Religious Aphorisms*, xxv.

the Holy Spirit, convicting the world of both sin and right-eousness (16:8-13). In three passages where Paul discusses one Spirit and giver of a diversity of gifts, he also develops the metaphor of one body and many parts (Romans 12:3-8; 1 Corinthians 12:1-31; Ephesians 4:1-16). As the "Head" of the church — the church being the "body" of Christ — our living Lord directs. But it is up to the distinctive members of the body to stay connected to the Head, to do their parts well, and to work in coordinated ways with other members of the body. This involves both individuality and mutuality.

On the other hand, while we do live in a post-denominational era, as a particular member of the larger body of Christ we have our own callings to carry out and functions to perform. Therefore, each "part" of the body must under-stand its role and place within Christ's work. Every role is not the responsibility of every part, but understanding one's func-tion and performing it well is central to edifying the rest of the body and serving Christ effectively. Therefore, Baptists, Meth-odists, Lutherans, Catholics, Pentecostals, and others should live into their own callings and serve their vocations well — likewise, Friends. Each part of the body of Christ must serve the body faithfully, thereby enhancing the Church's service to the world. As the One who walks among the lampstands in Revelation 2-3 reminds the churches of Asia Minor, each must play its assigned role effectively, lest its lampstand be removed and replaced by another.

A second feature of Paul's body-and-parts imagery for the church is that one part of the body cannot act in isolation; it must work in coordination and harmony with other parts and groups. The hand is not the foot, nor is the foot the ear; but each part needs the others, and each part ought to con-tribute to the success of the others as a central goal in serving its role effectively. Therefore, cooperation and mutuality are central to being a valued member of the larger movement. Friends must thus understand their roles and callings clearly and carry them out faithfully. They must also work for the success of other parts of the larger body of Christ, and such mutuality of service is central to being a contributing part of the church.

A third aspect of being an effective part of the larger body of Christ is to remain connected to the Head – Jesus Christ. When body parts are disconnected from the head, problems result such as dystrophy, spasms, retardation, hyperactivity, and numbness. Connected and energized responses to the central nervous system, however, make a part of the body an invaluable member and an irreplaceable extension of the Head. Therefore, in following Jesus effectively, each part of the larger body of Christ must understand and serve its functions and callings well. It must then coordinate with and edify other parts of the body and operate in ways receptive and responsive to the direction of the Head.

Perhaps Friends should see our calling not so much as a denomination of the larger whole, but more of an order – like those within the Catholic movement – which have been entrusted a full-time distinctive vocation in service to the larger church and the world beyond. If such is the case, the measure of success is not size but faithfulness.

As mentioned, while we live in a post-denominational era, each part has its own roles to play. George Fox emphasized that the "church" is not a building, but the people of God, and he pointed out that believers are "the church of which Christ was the head." In maintaining connectedness to the Head, in maximizing coordination with others, and in carrying out our callings effectively, the church of Christ is edified and the Lord's work is furthered. As Neave Brayshaw has well pointed out, the Society of Friends "has rediscovered, neither easily nor quickly, the truth that it exists not for itself, but for the world's healing."[7]

The Present Leadership of the Resurrected Lord

While Christians believe in the resurrection of Christ, too few have taken seriously what it means to live under his present leadership. In fact, the implications of believing in the resurrected Lord may be among the most neglected aspects of the Christian faith! Such neglect was one of the factors that spurred the missionary zeal of George Fox and other early Friends, who sought to spread the gospel of the living Lord to all parts of the earth, Christian and otherwise. The world still needs this message as much today as ever before. As George Fox put it in 1661:

> Dwell in the Power of Truth...every one in your Measures...feeling and knowing the Lord's Power everyone in yourselves...that you may sit down in your own possession of everlasting Life.
>
> In that meet together, waiting upon the Lord. In it keep your meetings, where you may feel the Chief Shepherd leading you into pastures of Life. And so, the blessing of the Lord be with you![8]

As suggested by this statement, the power of the resurrected Lord affects us individually and corporately. As indi-

---

7. *The Quakers*, (London: Friends Home Service, 1969), 348.

8. George Fox. *The Power of the Lord Is Over All: The Pastoral Letters of George Fox*, ed. T. Canby Jones (Richmond, IN: Friends United Press, 1989) Letter 203. Fox uses the word "measure" to refer to the special way each person is reached by God.

viduals we actually experience the power of the resurrection in our lives, and this is good news indeed! The powers of sin and death are rendered toothless by the life-producing dynamics of the resurrection. There is no habit, no weakness, no failure that cannot be healed and redeemed by the power of Christ working in our lives.[9] As well as transforming the individual, however, the power of the resurrected Lord also affects the corporate fellowship of believers, and this is where contemporary Christians often falter. Put simply, one of the greatest needs of the church today is to experience the dynamic leadership of Christ as its Head, but knowing how this happens effectively is not easy.

The urgency of this need startled me several years ago when the main speaker at a Friends pastors' conference challenged us to be "good shepherds of our flocks" and lead our churches through efficient decision-making processes. "A wrong decision is better than no decision," declared our speaker in slightly overstated terms. He then went on to expound the virtues of authoritarian styles of church leadership, borrowing heavily from "management-by-objective" trends in the corporate executive world.

This troubled me greatly as a young pastor. On the practical level, I had observed several churches being torn apart by pastoral leaders who, in trying to develop a working hierarchy (with themselves, of course, at the top), had either alienated others with leadership abilities or had discouraged the use of their gifts. Ironically, the very goal they sought to

---

9. Paul describes these two kinds of victories in Philippians 4:13, "I can do all things through him who strengthens me," and Romans 8:11, "If the Spirit of him who raised Jesus...dwells in you, he will give life to your mortal bodies..." (NRSV).

achieve—furthering Christ's healing ministry in the world—they hindered by the means they pursued to achieve that end.

While I was aware that authoritarian leadership often divides and discourages the flock, I was also aware that such models work well in some cases. There is much to be said for alleviating the time-consuming frustrations of decision making within the church. Many a pastor, clerk, elder, or committee chairperson has suffered needlessly at the hands of those who freely assign responsibility without also granting the authority to carry out one's assignments—a central problem our speaker addressed. Sometimes groups get so involved with debating the best means to an end that accomplishing an important goal is forever frustrated by trivial discussions.

On an ideological level, however, I was disturbed by the implication that Christ's leadership is limited to a human structure. The goal of pastoral leadership as portrayed in the New Testament seems less preoccupied with pastors being "the" shepherd, or even the "undershepherd," and more concerned with leaders pointing people to the True Shepherd—Christ himself. Nearly all of the exhortations to pastors and other leaders in the New Testament emphasize humble servanthood and exemplary faithfulness, following the lead of Christ.[10] Some leaders were even corrected because they had abused their positions of service.[11]

---

10. Such passages as John 10:10-12; 21:15-17; and 1 Peter 5:2-4 emphasize the importance of pastors (and elders) being good "shepherds" to the "flock" of Christ, imitating his sacrificial example.

11. The above passages clearly have Ezekiel 34 in mind, where the "shepherds of Israel" are scolded for feeding themselves and not the flock. In 3 John 9 "Diotrephes, who likes to put himself first..." (NRSV) is challenged for using his authority in a heavy-handed way, and in 1 Peter 5:3 the selfish interests of pastoral leaders are confronted.

Just as the goal of the vocal minister is not simply to be heard but for the living Word of Christ to be heard through his or her words, so the primary calling of the pastoral minister is not to do shepherding but to lead the flock to the nurturing-healing power of Christ—the true Shepherd of the sheep. Paradoxically, this is what makes the shepherding work of a pastor most effective. When one truly becomes the servant of the church, the most fruitful service he or she can provide is continually building the connections between believers and their living Lord.[12] Because Christ himself bridges the gap between us and God as our High Priest, there is no need for another.

"Yes, but how does this work?" one might ask. The quick answer is that it is an uncharted sojourn, a walk of faith. There are no guarantees, no pat answers. Nevertheless, we do not operate in the dark. The same Spirit who inspired the Scriptures speaks to us as we read them. And these Scriptures promise us that Christ's Spirit will be with us, will guide us, and will lead us into all truth.[13] This is the most striking implication of one's belief in the resurrected Lord. If Christ is alive, he seeks to lead us, and if he seeks to lead us, we can discern and obey his will.

Believing this is one thing; doing it effectively is another. Fortunately, throughout the history of the church, learnings from the past inform our approaches today, and several prin-

12. Being "servant of the church or meeting" describes a Quaker view of leadership well. Just as a leader must be given clarity regarding his or her assignments, he or she must also be released and empowered with the authority and means to carry them out (as described on the previous page). Authority does not need to be hierarchical to be effective. The most important factor is specificity: Is a person empowered to carry out the specific tasks assigned?

13. The five *paraklētos* passages of John 14–16 state clearly that the risen Christ is with us, guides us into all truth, reminds us of Jesus' teachings, and convicts the world of sin and righteousness. See also Matthew 18:18-20: Where two or three are gathered in Jesus' name, he is present in their midst.

ciples have been found to be trustworthy. On a personal level one can test one's "leadings" by asking the following questions:

Questions for Testing One's Leadings

1. "Is this leading in keeping with the teachings of the Scriptures?" The Spirit who inspired the Scriptures will not contradict the truths contained in the Bible. The Bible serves as an objective referent to check subjective leadings.

2. "Are there examples from the past that may provide direction for the present?" We, the body of Christ, can often evaluate Christ's leadership more clearly by hindsight, and such observations may provide parallels that inform present issues.

3. "Is a leading self-serving, or is it motivated by one's love for God and others?" Most false leadings are revealed to be selfishly motivated, or at least tainted with self-interest, even if the goal sounds noble. The will of Christ is always perceived more clearly from the foot of the cross, and as we release our needs to God, we find that we open ourselves to God meeting our needs in ways pleasing to him.

4. "Does it matter who gets the credit?" The kingdom of God is never limited to the petty "empires" humans build. These will crumble, but what is done for Christ and his truth will last. A great deal of good can be done when it doesn't matter who gets the credit.

5. "Is the ministry of Jesus being continued in what we do?" If the world sees Christ in our time, it will be through the men, women, and children who are his hands and feet in the world. To pray in Christ's name and according to his will implies taking the time to seek out and know his desires, and this is what makes us his "friends" (John 15:12-16).

Along with these individual questions there are corporate guidelines for discerning Christ's leadership among us, based on the teachings of Scripture and refined by experience. While voting may bring a discussion to a speedy conclusion, this does not necessarily mean that the group has sought—let alone found—the will of Christ. On the other hand, unwieldy and endless discussions may be brought to a more effective resolution when the group understands the nature of the corporate task at hand. The goal of decision making within the church is less a matter of deciding what to do and more a matter of listening for the still, clear voice of the risen Christ, who speaks in Spirit and in truth. Quakers have learned a great deal about how this happens and have much to share with others regarding practical suggestions for corporate decision making in the church. Some of these include the following:

Guidelines for Effective Corporate Decision Making[14]

1. Matters of community maintenance deserve to be relegated to working groups. Only matters that concern the direction of the entire community deserve the searching of all, although clearness for the concerns of individuals is also appropriately sought in the gathered meeting for worship.

2. The meeting for business is also a meeting for worship. In such a meeting the central question is neither "What is expedient?" nor "What is the group consensus?" but "What is the leading of Christ in our midst?" Prepare accordingly and allow times of prayer and quiet searching within the meeting itself.

---

14. These themes are probably less familiar, and this makes them all the more important. They may be useful for clerks and committee chairpersons to use corporately, as those present are asked to focus on the goal and character of the "gathered meeting for worship in which business is conducted." Many of these insights may be attributed to Dealous Cox, former clerk of Reedwood Friends Church. These guidelines were also published in the *Indiana Friend* and *Quaker Life* as well as *Evangelical Friend*.

3. All members who have something to say have the responsibility to share clearly, but having done so, to release their contributions to the larger sense of the meeting and leading of the Spirit. No individual possesses all of God's truth, and the contribution of each who has something to say is essential. To withhold one's truth is a "high crime" against the meeting and an affront to the Lord. It may have been the very piece needed to complete the puzzle. The clerk should invite insight from all perspectives in order for the issue and its implications to be understood clearly.

4. Where there is a conflict of perspective, the issue must be sorted until the genuine issue or issues of disagreement is or are clarified. Then, those who hold opposing views are called to distinguish between preference and conscience. If it is a matter of preference, you must release it to the meeting and not stand in its way. If it is a matter of conscience, hold to your conviction as long as it holds you. The prophetic voice often sings a solo, at least for a while.

5. Friends must agree to wait until there is clarity of leading and then support the decisions made in unity. When this happens, meetings begin to experience the exciting reality of Christ's present leadership, and the meeting is energized to move forward in the strength of unity. Speaking with a united voice depends on waiting long enough to receive a common sense of leading. Not only do we seek Christ's leading, but the Spirit of Christ also seeks to lead us into truth.

What a difference our belief in the resurrected Lord makes in our daily lives! It is important to believe that God has a plan for the direction of the local church. We can know and obey Jesus' leadings individually and corporately through the direction of the Holy Spirit. While the Bible teaches this clearly, amazingly few Christians (including Quakers) have put it into practice. The world needs this message, especially in the form of the changed and changing lives of men, women, and children who, as George Fox said, "feel the Chief Shepherd leading [them] into the pastures of life."

Attending, Discerning, Minding

When Jesus taught his disciples to pray, "Our Father in heaven, hallowed be your name. Your kingdom come. Your will be done, on earth as it is in heaven" (Matthew 6:9-10 NRSV), he was not just teaching them a poetic utterance to recite. He was describing God's burning desire for the world. God desires nothing short of a full human-divine partnership in which God's will and pleasure are carried out in the course of everyday life as perfectly on earth as they are in heaven.

This is the calling of all believers everywhere, and Friends have sought for three-and-a-half centuries to make that calling central to all we do. Whether one aspires to be a part of the Friends movement or not, this venture involves three parts: attending, discerning, and minding.

Attending

That's what we do in worship, both privately and corporately. What are your first thoughts in the morning? Do you say, "Good morning, Lord!" or "Good Lord; it's morning!"? Do you begin your day offering your life to God anew, rehearsing your commitments and obligations in the light of God's presence? Do you attend the gentle promptings of the Spirit throughout the day, seeking always to be responsive to what John Woolman called a "motion of love," which is the Holy Spirit?

Attending is also what we do in the gathered meeting for worship. In worship, we express our love for God and receive God's love for us. That's where transformation happens. In worship we may enjoy inspiring music and moving words, but our goal is to attend the living Word of God, which addresses us through the music, the spoken word, and ultimately, the silence. This is why our time of "communion after the manner of Friends" is so important. It is here—in this sacramental context—where our attending the transforming word of the present Christ becomes most acute. Here it is that we listen for, tune in to, and attend the life-giving Word of God.

Discerning

That's what we hope happens because of our attentiveness to the divine will. "Is this a divine impression, or just a new idea?" "Is this a message for me alone, or is it a leading for others too?" These are the sorts of questions that emerge as we seek to distinguish the Lord's promptings from otherwise worthy notions. Discerning happens as we identify the singular voice of God among the clamoring many—both inward and outward—and it begins and ends with the cross. When we lay our concerns and interests before the cross of Jesus, we begin to see with new eyes. And yet, this is a paradox. Only by dying do we live, and only by releasing do we obtain. As we release our interests back to God, we find ourselves better enabled to see persons and situations as Jesus would. Out of that renewed vision, then, emerge the seeds of discernment.

Minding

After we attend and discern the divine will, the question of obedience emerges. Will we also heed, and will we do so responsively? Minding the present leading, again, hinges upon an affirmative disposition toward God. The life lived in an ongoing *yes* toward God will always incline toward trust and obedience. Trust is central because it assumes God is at work in the world beyond what the eye can see. Obedience matters because it shows that one has developed a habitual pattern of attentive responsiveness to the Holy Spirit's promptings.

Jesus gave his followers the Lord's Prayer as a pattern to live. But the carrying out of the divine will as perfectly on earth as it is in heaven happens dynamically, not statically. God's will for humanity is neither a schedule, nor a blueprint, nor a list of legalisms. It is a spiritual and relational reality, which Friends and other believers have long embraced and sought to engage. It involves attending, discerning, and minding the present leadership of the resurrected Lord.

When this happens, all things indeed become new; and, the Lord's Prayer is *answered*.

"Let all nations hear the word by sound or writing. Spare no place, spare not tongue nor pen, but be obedient to the Lord God and go through the world and be valiant for the Truth upon earth; tread and trample all that is contrary under....And this is the word of the Lord God to you all, and a charge to you all in the presence of the living God: be patterns, be examples in all countries, places, islands, nations, wherever you come, that your carriage and life may preach among all sorts of people, and to them; then you will come to walk cheerfully over the world, answering that of God in every one." (**George Fox**, 1656)

"In this humanistic age we suppose man is the initiator and God is the responder. But the living Christ within us is the initiator and we are the responders. God the Lover, the accuser, the revealer of light and darkness presses within us. 'Behold, I stand at the door and knock.' And all our apparent initiative is already a response, a testimonial to His secret presence and working within us. The basic response of the soul to the Light is internal adoration and joy, thanksgiving and worship, self-surrender and listening." (**Thomas Kelly**, 1941)

"But you will receive power when the Holy Spirit has come upon you; and you will be my witnesses in Jerusalem, in all Judea and Samaria, and to the ends of the earth." (**Jesus**, Acts 1:8 NRSV)

"In this view we accept the commission of our blessed Lord as given in Matthew 28:18, 19 and 20th verses: 'And Jesus came to them and spake unto them saying, *All authority hath been given unto me in heaven and on earth. Go ye, therefore, and make disciples of all the nations, baptizing them into the name of the Father and of the Son and of the Holy Ghost; teaching them to observe all things whatsoever I commanded you, and, lo, I am with you always, even unto the end of the world.'"* (**The Richmond Declaration**, 1887)

Part II

Evangelism and Convincement

The Power of the Good News

The subject of Quakers and evangelism might come across as a shock to some, as it is sometimes claimed that Quakers do not proselytize. Evangelization, however, is not proselytization. *Evangel* means "good news," and Friends have always been about the sharing of good news. Indeed, the beginning of the Quaker movement in 1652 is recognized as the day when George Fox preached to a crowd of more than 1,000 for three hours, standing on a rock on Firbank Fell in Northwest England, proclaiming that Christ is come to teach his people himself. From that time on, the Valiant Sixty set off across Britain and to different parts of the world, traveling in twos—like the original followers of Jesus—sharing the good news of Christ with all.

Note the similarities with Jesus and his mission. Jesus began his ministry declaring the kingdom of God is at hand, calling for people to take notice, tune in, turn around, and believe in the good news. Following his death and resurrection, the apostles continued to proclaim that the power evident in his ministry, and the power that raised him from the dead, was available in the *here and now*, not only in the *there and then*. Likewise, as with all attempts to recover apostolic Christianity, George Fox and early Friends proclaimed the advent of the "Everlasting Gospel." The power-imbued message has never been about what Quakers can do or have done; it has always been about what God has done—and is now doing—through the risen Christ. George Fox introduced his collection of pastoral letters with these words:

> And I was sent to "turn people from darkness to the light" (Acts 26:1), which Christ, the second Adam, did enlighten them withal; that they might see Christ their Way to God with the Spirit of God, which he pours upon all flesh, that with it they might have an understanding to know the things of God, and to know him, and his Son, Jesus Christ, which is eternal Life; and so might worship the living God, their maker and creator, who takes care for all, who is Lord of all; and with the Light and Spirit of God they might know the Scriptures, which were given forth from the Spirit of God in the saints, and the holy men and women of God.[1]

We all too easily confuse the messenger with the message. When we think of great evangelistic movements, we often focus on bold individuals and the ways God used them and their efforts. Sometimes we remember also their frustrations and failures. However, the issue is not simply one of daunting ventures or keen training. These certainly help, but we must not equate the power of the evangelist with the power of the Evangel. The former implies human giftedness; the latter involves the ultimate gift of God.

Let's unpack those words a bit. The Greek word for "power" is *dunamis*—the same root as the word "dynamite."

---

1. George Fox. *The Power of the Lord Is Over All: The Pastoral Letters of George Fox*, ed. T. Canby Jones (Richmond, IN: Friends United Press, 1989), 1.

On the one hand, it simply means "ability"—the capacity to effect. On the other, it bears with it associations of explosive power which cannot be contained. To consider the power of the everlasting gospel is to be mindful of the explosive impact of God's breaking into human history with finality and life-changing effect. And this relates directly to what it means to be "evangelical," whether one is a Friend or not.

Further, the Greek word *evangelion* comes from two words: *eu*, meaning "happy," "pleasant," or "good;" and *angelia*, meaning "message" or "news." A common association in ancient contemporary literature involves the empowerment of receiving of the "good news" that a battle has been won, complete with its implications for allied individuals and communities. Receiving news of the completed action makes all the difference for the hearers. It means people can live differently and take up new outlooks and ventures. In short, "good news" orders a new way of being based on a world-changing declaration of what has happened in history, and implicitly beyond it.

May I introduce yet another word? While "kingdom" language feels out of date for us in our democratic societies, and it might even seem sexist to some or despotic to others, the Greek word *basileia* had a much broader meaning. It also meant "government" or "reign," or better yet, "leadership." It is the saving/revealing activity of God's leadership that Jesus came to inaugurate, and which Fox and others rediscovered many centuries later. As testified in Jewish Scripture as well, God is at work in the world, wanting to lead, heal, order, and restore all people to places of ultimate wholeness and joy. And, carrying out that mission on the Father's behalf, the Jesus of history continues to be at work in the world, even now, through the power and presence of the Holy Spirit, and in the changed and changing lives of Jesus' followers.

This good news changes everything in its path. It creates a new reality merely by its having been spoken. It addresses not "how" something has happened, nor "why," nor "where," nor "when." It simply declares *that* God has acted on our behalf—and is at work—making all things new. To put it in the words of George Fox, "Christ is come to teach his people himself," and "The power of the Lord is over all!" So what difference does the mere announcement of the gospel make for our lives today?

First, notice that it is not we who have acted or merited God's saving/redeeming action; it is *God* who has taken the first step toward us—an action rooted in divine love. As Paul puts it, it is by grace we are saved, not of ourselves, lest anyone should boast (Ephesians 2:8-9). This means the everlasting gospel is not a function of anyone's deservedness; rather, it is solely a factor of God's unmerited gift of love—grace. To consider this fact leads one to a sense of awe and humbled gratitude, welling up within anyone who takes notice, tunes in, turns around, and believes.

Second, the action toward us is loving, accepting, and healing—just what our lives need in order to be whole. None of us is complete within ourselves; rather, God's saving love completes us and brings us into a state of wholeness and well-being. Receiving the divine embrace, however, not only changes our lives, it also enables us to embrace others with the same unconditional warmth and love we have received from God.

Third, when we consider the good news that God has acted in ways saving, revealing, and healing toward us, we begin to anticipate unexpected ways God may be at work around us and within us. George Fox called these events moments of "visitation." As C. S. Lewis puts it in the first of his Narnia chronicles, "Aslan is on the move!" God is at work. Christ is here. The kingdom of God is upon us, among us, within us. Are we ready for moments of divine visitation? They may be closer than we think! As Francis Howgill testified of his experience:

The Kingdom of Heaven did gather us and catch us all, as in a net, and his heavenly power at one time drew many hundreds to land. We came to know a place to stand in and what to wait in; and the Lord appeared daily to us, to our astonishment, amazement and great admiration, insomuch that we often said one unto another with great joy of heart: "What, is the Kingdom of God come to be with men? And will he take up his tabernacle among the sons of men, as he did of old?"[2]

Of course, any sort of human-divine encounter may throw us into a flurry of inward questions: Is my house in order? Am I attentive to Christ's secret and subtle presence in my life, leading me away from sin and toward the ways of God? Do I heed the gentle promptings of the Holy Spirit, readily and faithfully? Am I sensitized to the awesome power and presence of God, which surrounds and fills us even more than the air we breathe? Do I find it easy to respond to God's saving/redeeming initiative in faith, trusting in what God has done rather than lesser alternatives? Are our lives becoming an ongoing *yes* to the leadership of the present Christ, even now at work within us as we read these words?

If some of these queries seem to take root in your heart, you are experiencing the power of the good news — even now! God is never absent but is here, waiting to be engaged. Throughout history, God has been at work — decisively and transformingly — and God is at work *even now*, in the present, making all things new. The business of our lives becomes the arena of God's redeeming action. When God's saving/ revealing presence is felt, our lives change. As the hymnwriter said, "Hearts unfold like flowers before Thee...Center of unbroken praise." (Henry Van Dyke)

The original message of Jesus and early Friends then and now is: "The present, powerful, and active leadership of

2. Francis Howgill, "Testimony Concerning Edward Burrough," in *Works of Edward Burrough* (London: William Warwick, 1662).

God is upon you, among you, and within you. Turn and believe in the good news." May we thus allow our lives to become an ongoing *yes* in response to God's *yes* to the world, whereby we not only hear the news, but we also embrace its transforming power and love. When that happens, we have not only heard the good news; it is something that we *become* to those around us.

Convincement Versus Coercion

Jesus says, "You will know the truth and the truth will make you free" (John 8:32 NRSV). Truth liberates precisely because it overcomes our bondage to darkness, sin, and self. The mere flickering of light extinguishes darkness, and Jesus' coming as the Light of the World brings the crisis of revelation into our lives. But Jesus liberates because he is the saving/revealing initiative of God — a contrast to everything that is of human origin, including religious platforms and schemes. In that sense, evangelism is foundationally a matter of convincement rather than coercion.

Several years ago I attended a "how-to" seminar on increasing the membership of the local church. The motto used a tongue-in-cheek slogan, "by hook or by crook," expanding on the gospel imagery of "fishers of men" (thus, the fisher's hook) and "shepherd of the sheep" (thus, the shepherd's crook).

The seminar actually made some very helpful points about how to share the gospel effectively, especially for unchurched audiences. The slogan, however, traded on a truism in a way that, while amusing, also made me uneasy. Too often people perceive or experience evangelism as coercion.

"By hook or by crook" evokes impressions of pressured attempts to "get" someone to do something against his or her will; as in physics, every action creates an equal and opposite reaction. Who knows how many would-be believers have refused to embrace the true gospel because of such misrepresentations of God's saving love? My belief is that Christ shows us a better way.

God sent us his Son because he loves us. Paul was constrained by the love of Christ to broadcast the good news (2 Corinthians 5:14), and such has been the central motivation of truly effective missionaries, from David Livingstone to John R. Mott to the missionary outreach of Friends over the last century and more. Likewise, authentic and effective evangelism is ever motivated by a sense of God's love for one another, which alone energizes the faithful evangelist's work. Our focus is always on God's love and its object (the world) rather than the channel (the evangelist) when we do evangelism well. Otherwise, if outreach becomes coercive, it ceases to be "news," let alone "good" news.

Convincement, on the other hand, relates to truth— God's truth. It implies the absence of human force, or even agenda, although thoughtful planning and organization are always in order. Authentic evangelism has to do with the revelation of God's saving/redeeming love and the human response of faith to it. When that happens, the evangelist has "succeeded," but she or he cannot take credit. It is God's truth that has prospered, of which human efforts are but a facilitative part.

So, how is one convinced of the truth, and how does one become a convinced believer? On the one hand, convincement of the truth involves simply receiving the good news that God has acted in history, lovingly extending the gift of grace to us—a gift we receive through faith alone. When we take it personally, believing that God extends his love and grace to us individually, in particular as well as globally, a new birth begins. According to John 3:3 in the NRSV, one cannot see the kingdom of God unless one is "born from above" (sometimes translated "born again"). So, being born from above begins with acknowledging God's saving/revealing work toward us, saying thank you, thereby receiving that unmerited gift by faith.

Another feature of being convinced of the truth is seeing our own condition as standing in need before God. The apostle Paul reminds us that all have sinned and come short of God's glory (Romans 3:23), and that the wages of sin is death (Romans 6:23), but most people need not be browbeaten into such an acknowledgment. Rather, the Holy Spirit—the Spirit of Truth—was sent by Christ to be with us and in us (John 14:17). The Spirit of Truth testifies to the words of Jesus as they are needed in our lives, guiding us into all needed truth (John 15:26; 16:13). More particularly, the Holy Spirit convicts (convicts and convinces are the same word in Greek) us of sin and of righteousness, so that we have no need of human measures, whether of others or our own (John 16:13). Because the Spirit of Christ, the Inward Teacher, leads us into truth about our true conditions—both challenging and affirming—we are opened to the liberating truth of Christ within.

Because spiritual convincement of our authentic condition—needy before God, and yet beloved of God—comes by revelation rather than human argumentation, the most effective evangelistic outreach is less a matter of apologetic bluster and more a factor of facilitating a transforming sense of the divine presence. Indeed, the apostle Paul was not "converted" on the road to Damascus by fine-sounding arguments; he was transformed by a direct encounter with the risen Lord, whereby he saw the error of his legalistic-though-zealous way (Acts 9). Like the callings of the prophets in Hebrew Scripture, an encounter with the living God leads to a spontaneous and humbled appreciation of one's woeful condition, which is then followed by God's redemptive action and the individual's receiving a mission and a message.

The gospel is thus not a compromise to offset God's otherwise stern set of legalisms. It is a grace-filled remedy to the human realities that no one has seen God at any time, and that despite the light that illumines all coming into the world (John 1:9), we often languish in darkness until we see the light clearly enough to embrace it. To use Gurney's imagery, whether the seeker has glimpsed a flickering candle or has beheld a noontide ray of the sun, the task of the evangelist is to add more light to light, and in doing so, to offer a gift rather than deliver an imposition.

This does not mean, however, that all who receive light will respond to it believingly. Some prefer darkness rather than light, lest their deeds be exposed as rooted in human origin rather than in God. But God did not send his Son to condemn the world; God sent his Son so that through him the world might be saved (John 3:17-21). And while some of his own did not receive him, those who believe receive the power to become children of God because they are born out of responding to the divine initiative, not the wiles or schemes of human ingenuity (John 1:11-13).

The obligation of the evangelist, then, becomes not the devising of an ingenious plan, but attending the leadings of the Holy Spirit as to how one is to share and "be" the good news most effectively. The Spirit provides openings no program ever could, and since the source of the Spirit's promptings is the redeeming love of God, evangelism rooted in the Spirit's movements of love will therefore be rooted in love.

Becoming a "convinced" believer in the truth of God is the essence of spiritual transformation. The light of Christ reveals, convicts, purifies, comforts, instructs, and empowers the believer as Jesus becomes Savior and Lord. The truth sets us free, and just as Jesus is the way, the truth and the life, he also is that light who coming into the world illumines all persons (John 14:6; 1:9). In that sense, the good news ceases to be an abstract notion for one to consider; it becomes a person for one to encounter. When that happens, we not only are confronted with the truth, we become *convinced* of it in a life-changing way.

Answering 'That of God' in Everyone

Are people sinners because they sin, or do they sin because they are sinners? The first view (argued by Pelagius around the turn of the fourth and fifth centuries) calls for people to resist sin and thereby overcome it; the second view (argued by Augustine) affirms that the fall of humanity is real, and that there is no hope for humanity outside of God's provision of grace. Put otherwise, Pelagius called for abandoning the first Adam's rebellion against God in exchange for imitating Christ's faithfulness; Augustine argued that the sin nature of Adam is real for all people, and that humanity's only hope is in solidarity with the Second Adam (Christ) and becoming a new creation, which comes by receiving grace alone through faith.

The second view won the day in the early church, leading to a doctrine of "original sin" and pointing to humans' absolute need of God's saving grace. In other words, "it is possible not to sin" lost and "it is impossible not to sin" won. While the fall of humankind is real (in Adam's sin we all sinned), humans are also first created good (in the divine image of God)—a biblical doctrine we often miss. Note the tension between human incapacity to live up to God's righteous standards, therefore requiring the gift of God's grace, and the belief that God is at work within the individual, therefore affirming "original goodness" as well as the reality of the fall.

John 14:6 declares that Jesus Christ is the only way to the Father, and yet John 1:9 affirms that the light of Christ, enlightening all, has come into the world; any who respond to God's light and love receive grace and become the children of God. Romans 3:10 declares that none are righteous—not even one—and yet Romans 2:14 affirms that even the Gentiles have a law unto themselves, pointing the way to God if they would but follow it. So the reality of our needy condition before God stands, as we cannot attain God's standards or merit God's love on our own. Yet God is also at work—at least potentially—within the lives of all people, so that makes a difference as to how we receive, understand, and share the gospel. Here Friends make a valuable contribution to ways we think about God's saving/revealing work in the world.

When George Fox coined the term "that of God" in people's consciences, he often made reference in his surrounding text to the light of Christ within, or God's law written on the hearts of Gentiles. While some might speak of "the inner light" or "my light" as a way of affirming individuality, Fox and early Friends did not see illumination as originating with the individual; it was the "Light of Christ" encountered inwardly (hence the correctly used term—"the *inward* light") that they connected with the saving, revealing, guiding work of Christ. Likewise, appeals to God's workings within the human conscience build upon Paul's teachings on the natural law within, although Paul's main point in Romans 1–2 is that all stand convicted and in need of God's grace—Jew and Gentile alike—so that all are in need of God's provision of grace through Christ.

So how do we "answer that of God" in the lives of others? For one thing, our acknowledgment of God's presence with others helps us see people as having real access to God's truth, even the light of Christ within, assuming that God has already been at work within the other's heart and conscience. Therefore, whether or not a person knows the outward story of Jesus, the divine light of Christ has arrived there first, and the calling of God's love for the world connects God's love within us to Christ's light within the other. That's what directs conversation and concern as we seek to be extensions of God's presence and grace to those we meet. A youth minister I knew would simply ask kids he met, "So, how are things with you and God?" Out of hundreds of conversations, no one ever failed to understand the question, and no one ever rejected it; many found the conversation helpful in leading into a deeper relationship with God, which most people want. So regarding all persons as having access to the enlightening work of Christ within allows outreach and contacts to be rooted in loving concern for the other, making us first listeners rather than speakers. That in itself is a miracle of grace! Answering always follows hearing, and hearing usually follows listening.

A second thing that happens as we seek to "answer" that which is "of God" in the other is that our focus changes from agendas or human strategies to simply focusing on the spiritual heart of the other. Beyond words, we find ourselves attending the feelings of others. What are *their* concerns? How are *they* feeling led? How are inward and outward challenges fulfilling or thwarting *their* callings and hopes in life? God is at work in all these concerns — within others and within ourselves. In that sense, we share a pilgrimage as seekers of the truth and believers that God's provision and guidance are real. Even conversation with a so-called "enemy" is transformed radically when we address that person's engagement with God's truth within his or her own conscience. At the heart of effective peace work is believing that persons on all sides of all conflicts have access to the God of peace, who works in people's hearts — at least potentially — providing ways out of conflicts and impasses if we will but attend his leadings.

Finally, as we seek to answer that which is from God, at work in the consciences of all people, including those with

whom we serve on committees or meet in the marketplace—
we find our discourse and witness changing. What we have to
share thus becomes less about ourselves and more of a testimony to the grace and power of God working within us—a
deeply humbling consideration. As William Penn said of early
Quaker ministers, "They were changed men [and women]
themselves before they went about to change others. Their
hearts were rent as well as their garments, and they knew the
power and work of God upon them."[3] A calling to share about
God's love involves first a calling to abide in that love and
being willing, then, to speak from firsthand experience about
what one knows personally.

When that happens, according to Fox, faithful witnesses
to Christ will not only be a blessing to those around us, but
they will also be a blessing to God: "Then you will come to
walk cheerfully over the world, answering that of God in everyone; whereby in them you may be a blessing, and make the
witness of God in them to bless you; then to the Lord God you
shall be a sweet savor, and a blessing."[4] May it ever be so!

On Being
Great Commission Quakers

Soon after George Fox preached a life-changing, three-hour
message on top of a large rock on Firbank Fell, the Valiant
Sixty set off to reach the world for Christ. They went with
nothing but the message that Christ has come to teach his peo-

---

3. William Penn, *The Rise and Progress of the People Called Quakers* (Philadelphia:
   Friends Book Association, 1905), 45-46.

4. George Fox, Journal of George Fox, ed. Nickalls (Philadelphia: Philadelphia
   Yearly Meeting, 1985), 263.

An earlier version of "On Being Great Commission Quakers" was published in
Evangelical Friend in 1992.

ple himself! The days of the apostles were alive again, and Christ was calling any and all who would be faithful to go and to be agents of the gospel. Later, while Fox was imprisoned in Scarborough Castle in 1665, Lord Falconbridge, governor of Tinmouth Castle, challenged Fox to respect political and religious leaders—members of Parliament, bishops, and priests. Fox said he did indeed respect all ministers who were truly like those whom Christ sent:

> ...Such as were qualified, and were in the same power and spirit the apostles were in. But such bishops and teachers...I did not acknowledge; for they were not like the apostles. For Christ said to his ministers, "Go you into all nations, and preach the gospel;" but you members of parliament, who keep your priests and bishops in such great fat benefices [payment for services rendered], have spoiled them all. For do you think they will go into all nations to preach? Or will go any farther than a great fat benefice? Judge yourselves whether they will or not.[5]

Note that Fox here distinguishes authentic ministers of Christ from imposters by examining willingness to follow the Great Commission of Christ and to spread the good news around the world, making disciples of all nations (Matthew 28:19-20). Indeed, the greatest growth of the Quaker movement is characterized by two primary epochs: the first generation of the Friends movement and the Friends missionary movements in the twentieth century, the latter of which have led to larger numbers of Friends in Africa and Latin America than in Britain and North America. In both cases, Friends were willing to become Great Commission Quakers.

In the freshman Bible class I teach, students and I explore the similarities and differences between the four Gospels, and almost every semester one of my students asks,

---

5. Fox, *Journal*, 1666. Of course, released ministries also face risks of hireling tendencies.

"Why is the 'Great Commission' mentioned in all four Gospels?" As students learn, the Great Commission appears within each of the four Gospels, and yet in different, fascinating ways.

Rather than hearing a "monophonic" recording of Jesus' command to his followers, hearing the Great Commission in each of the four Gospels is like listening to a "quadraphonic" rendition of it, as each of the Gospel writers complements the others with his own distinctive perspective. This also means that one's understanding of Jesus' Great Commission in the New Testament will be fullest if one explores its renditions in all four Gospels, rather than in just one.

Before delving into this, let's consider similarities of the Great Commission in all four Gospels. Notice the same features in all four accounts:

1. First, the Great Commission is declared by the resurrected Lord. This means that it reflects early Christians' understandings of how the Church was to continue the very work and ministry Jesus had begun. Further, it represents their understandings of Christian discipleship in the light of the death and resurrection of Jesus Christ. Often we read in the Gospels that the disciples were a bit "fuzzy" (my paraphrase) about what Jesus meant—until after the resurrection, when all things became clear. The Great Commission is a prime example of that clarified comprehension. It represents the early Christians' understandings of how they were to continue the work of Jesus as commissioned by the risen Lord.

2. Within all four Gospels, Jesus' command is portrayed as a "last will and testament." It motivates Jesus' would-be followers by declaring his final intention for their lives. Jesus leaves no room for ambiguity or second-guessing. His words are directive. Clear. They call for responsive obedience to his mandate. In that sense, the articulation

of Christian mission becomes a "commission," as the hearer of the Word "comes alongside" Jesus as a partner in furthering his mission.

3. In each case, the commissioning message of Jesus is "translated" for a specific Christian audience, reflecting the understanding of the Gospel writer and the specific needs of his situation. As Everett Cattell said:

> It is clear that before his ascension and in different places he discussed this subject and the whole of those discourses has not been recorded. Different disciples were struck by one or another part of his message and preserved those portions which impressed them most.[6]

This is one of the things that makes Bible study exciting! As we explore the similar and yet distinctive ways in which the Gospels articulated the Great Commission within the early Church, our understandings of Christian mission today become enriched. We may even detect a progression of theme that clarifies for us what the Lord's commission involves for his followers today.

Now we turn to looking at the distinctive elements in the four Gospel renditions.

Mark

The Great Commission in Mark is described like this: *Go and preach the gospel to all creation.* Mark was the first Gospel written (probably around 70 AD), and it usually gives us a good impression of Christian understandings about Jesus in the middle first century. However, the Great Commission in Mark appears in Mark 16:15, which is included in a section (Mark 16:9-20) not found in the earliest Greek manuscripts. Nevertheless, despite significant differences of style and nuance, the commissioning words of Jesus here are remarkably similar to

---

6. *Christian Mission* (Richmond, IN: Friends United Press, 1981), 1.

Mark's emphases upon being sent and proclaiming the good news.

John the Baptist "kicks off" the ministry of Jesus, having been sent by God to prepare the way for the Lord (Mark 1:3). After John was imprisoned, Jesus' ministry comes into its own: "The time is fulfilled, and the kingdom of God has come near; repent, and believe in the good news" (Mark 1:15 NRSV). He calls his first four disciples to leave their nets and to follow him (Mark 1:16-20). He appoints the Twelve to be with him and to proclaim the gospel (Mark 3:14-19), and then sends them out two by two to preach repentance, to drive out demons, and to heal the sick (Mark 6:7-13). It is not surprising, therefore, that even in Mark's "second ending," the command to "go and preach" is central. It represents the apostolic sense of urgency the first Christians must have felt in their mission to spread the gospel. Regardless of the receptivity of the "soils" or the fate of the "seed" (Mark 4:3-20), Christians are to broadcast the Word—the seed of the gospel—thus continuing the mission and message of Jesus.

Luke/Acts

The Great Commission in Luke/Acts goes like this: *Stay [tarry] until you are filled with power; then you will be my witnesses.* To the mandate "go and preach," Luke adds the indispensable factor of divine empowerment. The closing scenes of Luke dovetail into the opening scenes of Acts—like a feature movie and its climactic sequel! In Luke 24:49 Jesus commands the disciples to wait, to tarry in the city until they are clothed with power from on high. After leading them to Bethany, Jesus lifts up his hands and blesses them before ascending into heaven (Luke 24:50-51). At once, their response is to become consumed in worship, joy, and praising God (Luke 24:52-53). Indeed, they are filled with and immersed in the Holy Spirit (Acts 1:4-5).

The book of Acts, however, adds the implication of such encounters: To be changed by Christ is to be commissioned by Christ. "But you will receive power when the Holy Spirit has come upon you; and you will be my witnesses in Jerusalem, in all Judea and Samaria, and to the ends of the earth " (Acts 1:8 NRSV). Indeed, the rest of Acts documents the fulfillment of this prediction. The Christian movement grows with unassailable force—first locally, then regionally, then nationally, and finally, globally. But the central factor according to Luke is the empowering force of the Holy Spirit.

Without the Spirit the church is impotent. How often well-meaning Christians are tempted to start a missions project, fully enthused and equipped with a solid strategy, but without having *waited* on the Lord until being filled with power from on high. Luke reminds us that the success of spiritual mission always hinges upon spiritual empowerment, and this comes from prayerful waiting on the Lord.

Matthew

The Great Commission in Matthew declares: *Go and make disciples of all nations.* Just as Luke contributes the empowerment of the Spirit, Matthew adds the community-building motifs to Mark's terse "go and preach." As Luke and Acts were probably written in the 80s of the first century, Matthew was probably written around 90 AD, as the church faced making the transition from being a growing movement to becoming a larger institution. The church-building interest of Matthew is clear from several examples: (A) Only Matthew's Gospel mentions the word *ecclēsia* (church). (B) Matthew 16:17-19 outlines the institutional means by which Peter (and Jesus?) will be succeeded. (C) Matthew 18:15-35 emphasizes the importance of accountability, proper church discipline procedure, and the necessity of seasoning authority with a spirit of forgivingness and grace. It is therefore not surprising at all that Matthew is interested in the discipling work of the church. Rather than simply going and preaching, the Christian emissary is commanded to go and "make disciples of all nations" (Matthew 28:19).

Notice that the discipling process is described as having two basic functions: induction and education. New believers are to be baptized "in the name of the Father and of the Son and of the Holy Spirit," and the main point here is that by means of Christ's authority (Matthew 28:18), their admission to the new community is confirmed with divine finality. To interpret the emphasis to be water baptism here (a Jewish ritual adapted somewhat variably by early Christians) instead of what it symbolized (meaningful inclusion in the Christian community) is to miss the point and to reduce the Great Commission to ritualism. John's baptism signified the turning from the world and repentance from sin. Jesus' baptism, on the other hand, involves being immersed in the Holy Spirit (Acts 1:5; 19:1-6; John 1:33; 3:5-8), and this is what confirms one's membership in the family of God (John 1:12).

It is often wrongly assumed that Quakers don't believe in baptism. But we do, and radically so. One cannot live the Christian life without being transformed by the baptism of Jesus, which is with fire and the Holy Spirit (Matthew 3:11; Mark 1:8; Luke 3:16; John 1:26-34; Acts 11:16). Water prefigured this spiritual immersion, and even came to symbolize it within the Christian movement. But Jesus apparently did not employ water baptism (John 4:2), and water baptism should never be confused with the "real thing" — an abiding immersion in the Spirit which Christ alone can offer. This spiritual reality is what Paul described as the "one baptism" (Ephesians 4:5), the baptism of Jesus, which is elsewhere contrasted to that of John.

After initiation follows education. Notice that Jesus is not portrayed here as simply extending "best wishes" to the spiritual infant before abandoning him or her to the task of maturation. No. He commands his followers to teach, just as they have been taught by him. In this way, the new believer grows into maturity and the church becomes strengthened in its conviction. Virtually everywhere the church thrives, it thrives because it has become able to introduce new Christians into the community of faith successfully, and because it has learned to prepare people for ministry effectively. This is what it means to make disciples of all nations.

John

The Great Commission in John is emphatic: *As the Father has sent me, so I send all of you.* John's is the "apostolic gospel." Rather than leaving the role of apostleship to an "office" or to a church hierarchy, John takes great pains to emphasize Jesus' imbuing all of his followers with apostolic mission. The Greek word *apostolos* means "one who is sent," and Jesus extends his own divine commission to include his followers. To be an apostle is to have encountered Jesus Christ and to be sent by him. Thus, the invitation to follow him is, at the same time, a calling to be sent by him—as his "friends," who know the Master's business and who are responsive to his leadings (John 15:14-15).

Notice the apparent correctives to rising institutionalism in the late-first-century Christian movement (John 20:21-23):

- Apostolicity is extended to "the many," not just "the few" (v. 21). Far from an elitist appeal for a few super-Christians or a martyr plea to labor in the fields of service "unrewarded," this is John's portrayal of Jesus involving all of his followers in Christian mission. In this sense, apostolic Christianity lives today! To encounter the Spirit of the risen Lord is to be commissioned and sent by him, and this is the spiritual essence of true apostolic succession.

- Jesus "breathed on" (inspired) the disciples and declared, "Receive the Holy Spirit" (v. 22 NRSV). Rather than imbuing an "office" or a ceremony with God-breathed authority or efficacy, Jesus fills the disciples with his Spirit by the mere fact of his presence. (See also Matthew 18:20.) He also promises to lead them into all truth through his comforting and convicting presence within the gathered meeting, and this is the basis for their sense of peace (John 14:25-27; 16:7-15; 20:19).

- Jesus gives them the responsibility—not just the privilege—of being agents of forgiveness and reconciliation in the world (John 20:23). Just as the role of apostle is expanded from the few to the many, so is the priesthood of believers. As a contrast to Matthew 16:19 and 18:18, the privilege/responsibility of extending God's saving forgiveness is given to all of Jesus' followers, not just Peter and his successors. In this sense, the healing/ saving work of Jesus is multiplied by the number of his followers who heed the call and accept the commission.

Just as George Fox saw the willingness to embrace the Great Commission as a measure of authentic Christian ministry, a sense of mission is what makes a difference in the vitality of the Church. Emil Brunner said, "The Church exists by mission, just as fire exists by burning."[7] When we consider the Great Commission in all four Gospels, we get a fuller picture—or a quadraphonic rendition—of what our Christian mission ought to be like today. It involves going and preaching; waiting on the filling of the Holy Spirit; making disciples of all nations; and embodying the apostolic, inspired, priestly ministry of Jesus himself. Perhaps this is what Paul had in

---

7. *The Word and the World* (London: SCM Press, 1931), 108.

mind when he declared that all creation groans in eager expectation for the revelation of the children of God (Romans 8:19). As we encounter the risen Lord and are commissioned by him to continue his saving/revealing work in the world, the incarnation happens anew. We indeed become Jesus' hands and feet, furthering work he came to do.

What Canst *Thou* Say?

Margaret Fell describes one of her first encounters with George Fox as an experience that caused her to sink into her pew and to weep as one who had been "cut to the heart." She later reported, "I cried in my spirit to the Lord, 'We are all thieves, we are all thieves, we have taken the Scriptures in words and know nothing of them in ourselves.'" Several were "convinced of the truth" that day, and despite attempts to arrest him, George Fox continued in his evangelistic ministry. Fell commented later: "I saw it was the truth, and I could not deny it...but I desired the Lord that I might be kept in it, and I desired no greater portion." The message she reported hearing from Fox was this:

> Then what had any to do with the Scriptures, but as they came to the Spirit that gave them forth. You will say, Christ saith this, and the apostles say this, but what canst thou say? Art thou a child of the Light and hast walked in the Light, and what thou speakest, is it inwardly from God?[8]

From this encounter we see something central to spiritual authority. Rather than being a factor of citing secondhand

---

8. "The Testimony of Margaret Fell Concerning Her Late Husband." Appendix to *The Journal of George Fox, Vol. 2* (London: Edward Hicks [Friends Tract Association], 1891 [1694]), 512-513.

authorities (religious officials, authoritative texts, prescribed creeds—even witty quips or engaging illustrations), spiritual authority is a direct factor of personal spiritual experience. It cannot be otherwise. It is not knowledge about the Deity that matters; it is intimate acquaintance with God that counts. Of course, thinking about what it means to know God and to live in ways pleasing to God (theology) is important, and this may even deepen and enhance one's relationship with God. But there is no replacement for a deep and abiding experiential relationship with God when it comes to authentic spirituality.

On this score, Friends have borne faithful witness to the immediacy of Christ—present in the world and drawing all persons to himself, if they would but allow it. In so doing, they follow the example of the apostles, whose ministries were effective because they had spent time with Jesus (Acts 4:13). Likewise, Jesus came teaching directly a prophetic message from God, and the exclamation of the crowds was that he taught not as the scribes and Pharisees (citing human authorities or religious legitimation), but that he spoke with spiritual authority (Matthew 7:29). In calling for firsthand spiritual experience, Friends sought to uphold the teaching and example of the Lord. Describing his firsthand encounter with the living Christ, George Fox testifies: "And this I came to know experimentally."

One of the ways George Fox put this concern was to declare that being "bred at Oxford or Cambridge" does not fit one to be a minister of the gospel. The point is not that theological education is irrelevant. The point is that it can never be enough. Jesus called his first followers to be "with him" (Mark 3:14), and such is the first priority of discipleship in every generation. Likewise, Robert Barclay's *Apology* was for the "true Christian divinity," and this authoritative power results not from having a graduate degree in the subject—as important as rigorous preparation for ministry is — but from a transforming encounter with the risen Lord. There's no substitute for that! Jesus' words in John 17:3 provided the biblical basis for Barclay's *Apology* for authentic spirituality, affirming that the source of spiritual life is the intimate knowledge of God. Such is the true source and subject of all religious authority.

Another feature of the question, "What canst thou say?" is to take seriously our personal stories of how God has been at work in each of our lives. As mentioned earlier, God has no grandchildren; each of us must encounter anew the life-changing workings of the Holy Spirit in the here and now. Of course, this implies that God has indeed been at work in our lives and that we are aware of it. Each of us must therefore be receptive and responsive to Christ as the initial launching of an intentional journey of faith; yet, every day also bears within itself the opportunity for renewing that commitment in an ongoing way. This is what it means to become an authentic child of the Light.

The question thus becomes one of how well we do at walking in the Light, building on initial responses of faith, and continuing into Christian maturity. As we seek to follow Jesus in a firsthand adventure, we walk by faith, not by sight. No matter what questions people may raise with us, we testify with lived authority that Christ has indeed been at work within us, and this experiential witness becomes evidence that demands a verdict within the faith quests of others. It becomes our personal testimony that Christ can change, and is changing, the world one life at a time — beginning with our own.

All of this relates to the source and character of what we have to share. Is it simply from us, or is its root the prompting and workings of the Holy Spirit within us? Is it inwardly from God, or is it of creaturely origins? When experiential encounter with Christ becomes the measure for what we offer as a witness, that narrows it down a good deal. The leadings of

Christ rightly supplant human agendas and interests, and what we share freely is what we have freely received from Christ, for he is both the source and the goal of all authentic Christian witness and ministry. The focus ceases to be upon ourselves and remains fixed upon what Christ is doing. After all, knowing what the Master is doing and following attentively his lead (John 15:14-15) is what makes people Jesus' friends!

"Now was I come up in spirit through the flaming sword into the paradise of God. All things were new, and all the creation gave another smell unto me than before, beyond what words can utter." **(George Fox,** 1647)

"Not by strength of arguments...came [I] to receive and bear witness of the Truth, but by being secretly reached by Life. For, when I came into the silent assemblies of God's people, I felt a secret power among them, which touched my heart; and as I gave way unto it I found the evil weakening in me and the good raised up; and so I became thus knit and united unto them, hungering more and more after the increase of this power and life whereby I might feel myself perfectly redeemed; and indeed this is the surest way to become a Christian." **(Robert Barclay,** 1676)

"The first gleam of light, 'the first cold light of morning' which gave promise of day with its noontime glories, dawned on me one day at Meeting, when I had been meditating on my state in great depression. I seemed to hear the words articulated in my spirit 'Live up to the light thou hast, and more will be granted thee.' Then I believed that God speaks to a man [and woman and child] by His Spirit. I strove to lead a more Christian life, in unison with what I knew to be right, and looked for brighter days; not forgetting the blessings that are granted to prayer." **(Caroline Fox,** 1841)

"But the hour is coming, and is now here, when the true worshipers will worship the Father in spirit and truth, for the Father seeks such as these to worship him. God is spirit, and those who worship him must worship in spirit and truth." **(Jesus,** John 4:23-24 NRSV)

Part III

Worship and Transformation

Transforming Worship

Transforming worship is both impressive and expressive. As we receive God's love for us and return our love for God, we find ourselves changed, transformed, renewed from the inside out. New insights come as to how we might live in the newness of life. Greater sensitivities emerge as we view those around us through the eyes of Jesus. We receive power to overcome life's challenges and temptations. All things indeed become new and, to use George Fox's imagery, creation even takes on another smell!

Friends have struggled, however, to find the right balance between impressive and expressive aspects of worship. Where liturgical Anglicans and preachy Puritans sought to influence by means of inputs and outputs, in Fox's day Quakers sought to bring a word from the Lord: Christ is the one to be listened to through and beyond outward forms, not the preacher nor the mass alone. And, as Christ is the one who desires to minister to others through human instruments, the minister and worshiper alike should attend Christ's leadings

An earlier version of "Transforming Worship" was published in *Evangelical Friend* in 1994.

first, instead of wishing to be seen or heard humanly. That is what makes worship a human-divine encounter instead of an audience-performance event (a mere "creaturely" activity).

As Friends entered their third and fourth generations, however, an overly conservative interest in not speaking beyond one's leading evolved into an age of Quietism. This is understandable; the excess of James Nayler and the suffering of persecution called for a more measured approach to enthusiasm. During this era the expressive aspect of worship was diminished and quiet waiting on the Lord developed into its classic forms among Friends. Within a century and a half, when young progressives began to use music in worship and emphasized the need for greater familiarity with and use of the Scriptures, Friends began to recover the expressive side of worship. For the last century or more, evangelical Quakers have refined the expressive arts of singing, preaching, and testifying, but silence has become a distant companion. We don't want to become quietistic, worshiping the silence; yet we ponder how recovering its use can be vitalizing, not deadening. An insight or two may help.

First, open worship at times suffers from a devastating mixture of expectations between what Wesleyans might call "testimonials of progress" and what Quakers might call "waiting in holy expectancy." In the testimony meeting the query is: "How has Jesus Christ made a difference in *your* life this week?" Any silence or pause bespeaks spiritual failure. Nobody wants that! So they search for some account of spiritual progress to share, and the fuller the meetings are, the greater the sense of success. These meetings can be very heart warming and encouraging, especially when the sharing is genuine and the progress real. One can understand how Wesleyans and Friends have historically joined others in revivalist ventures, seeking to restore accountability and vitality to the spiritual life of individuals and communities alike.

Conversely, the goal of expectant waiting on the Lord is to create the space wherein the living voice of Christ can be attended, heard, and obeyed. Because silence is fragile, busied contributions may distract the worshiper and frustrate the listening process. It also takes some time for the "chaff" to separate from the "wheat" of one's life. The rustlings of those with allergies to silence, or the well-meaning offerings of those who misjudge their offering's value, at times ensure a minimal level of contact with the streams of living water that flow from the deep currents of the Holy Spirit. However, a single taste of that deep refreshment makes one thirst for the true fountain and hunger for heavenly manna. One can endure a dozen dry runs for the memory and hope of the life-changing encounter with the present Christ, who speaks order into the chaos of our lives, and healing to the agonies of our souls. Silence cannot save, but the one we meet in it and through it saves if we let him.

Because these two wonderful and yet incompatible uses of open worship are often attempted at the same time, frustration inevitably occurs. The enthusiast speaks too often or too long for the meditator, and each misunderstands or undervalues the other's aspiration. One way forward is simply to be clear what kind of open worship is being cultivated during a particular time and setting. Friends may even wish to designate special times for testimony sharing and other times for expectant waiting, if both are desired. Then, with a bit of teaching and modeling by elders, the rest of the meeting will follow and the Lord will bless. Or, simply being aware of the tension can lead to greater sensitivity to the Spirit rather than focusing on an approach.

An additional point follows: Why save the life-changing invitation for the last five minutes of an already-full service? Why not make the entire meeting for worship a time to receive and respond to the living voice of Christ? "Just as I am... I come" is sung far more powerfully at the beginning of a meeting than at the end alone. Oh, that Christ would have an entire hour — or more — to melt our pride, lift our eyes, and mold our character on a regular basis! In silence, our props for distraction and symbols of worth come crashing down, until we are left with the naked truth about ourselves, if we dare face it. Few need silence more than those least comfortable with it. But out of the painful truth comes the power of life, and seeing our true dependence upon God for everything is the secret of recovering one's spiritual first love. That is where spiritual rebirth happens, again and again.

We evangelical Quakers have grown adept at doing expressive worship meaningfully, but to recover the fire of Pentecost and the glory of the burning bush, we must recover the impressive side of worship. However, such will not come by mastering formlessness as a new form. Our only hope is in *the real thing*: transforming encounter with none other than Jesus Christ, himself, through the power of the Holy Spirit. He has promised to be present in the gathered meeting, and prayerful preparation during the week imbues the meeting with holy expectancy. If we really believe that Christ is present where two or three are gathered in his name (Matthew 18:18-20), let us create the space to attend, hear, and obey his life-producing word. Jesus offers us manna from heaven, and he *is* that which he offers.

The Life of Devotion

Powerful corporate worship hinges upon vital private worship. Jesus departed from the crowds many a time to pray. Think of it! If Jesus set aside times for prayer, how much more ought we to do the same? No deep life of the Spirit, no empowerment from the Holy Spirit, no effective imitation of Christ is possible without cultivating a meaningful life of devotion. And yet, we find it all too easy to pass it over, looking for something more "relevant" or "practical" to be doing. But nothing is more practical or relevant than spending "useless" time with the Master. Between the busied industry of Martha in serving the Lord and the unhurried desire of Mary to spend time with the Lord, Luke 10:42 credits the example of Mary as the better way. We might be impressed at the energy and spiritual vitality of George Fox, as though he were exceptional, but William Penn understood the secret of his empowerment:

> Above all, George Fox excelled in prayer. The inwardness and weight of his spirit, the reverence and solemnity of his address and behaviour, and the fewness and fulness of his words have often struck even strangers with admiration as they used to reach others with consolation. The most awful, living, reverend frame I ever felt or beheld, I must say, was the prayer of George Fox. And truly it was a testimony. He knew and lived nearer to the Lord than other men, for they that know Him most will see most reason to approach Him with reverence and fear.[1]

But how do we "excel in prayer," develop "weight of spirit," express a "fewness and fullness of words," and "live near to the Lord" in ways that are life-changing for ourselves and reaching others with consolation? Part of it comes from simply following our desire for God and privileging spiritual hunger and thirst over others. As the psalmist says, "As a deer longs for flowing streams, so my soul longs for you, O God" (Psalm 42:1 NRSV). Then again, any sustained endeavor requires devotion and preparation, yet how do we embrace or celebrate a spiritual discipline without becoming slaves to routines and methods? While each of us must adopt an

---

1. William Penn in *Journal of George Fox*, ed. John L. Nickalls (Philadelphia: Philadelphia Yearly Meeting, 1985), xliv.

approach that fits our lives and demands most effectively, Friends have discovered several principles that may help. These are by no means unique to Friends, but they are indeed part of a long heritage of spiritual formation that deepens any who choose to travel the path. Consider a few guidelines:

Make your walk with Christ the center of your life and the priority of your day.

If you were to accord equal weight to the life of the Spirit as you do other ventures of life, how would that affect the order of your day? Do you find time to eat? Do you make time for sleep? Most of us can. And yet, when we consider our spiritual needs, how meager we tend to be in the apportionment of our time and energy toward *sustaining and deepening the life of the Spirit!* All hunger and desire are shadows of the more basic human desire, which is for relationship with the Divine. Paltry apportionments of time and energy for cultivating the life of the Spirit reflect not an ordering of our lives according to our true needs, but a lack of awareness of our most basic needs, central of which is the spiritual.

If our walk with Christ were to become the priority of our day, what would that mean for the ways we use our time and the quality of our attentiveness to the life of devotion? It could involve some radical changes. This foundational step of prioritizing our walk with Christ is far more important than selecting a particular plan or a method. As one becomes *given* to Christ, totally and unreservedly, ways of deepening that relationship tend to emerge as we become mindful of our conditions and what we truly need. As Saint Augustine reminds us well in his *Confessions,* "Thou hast made us for Thyself, O Lord, and our hearts are restless until they rest in Thee."

Set prime times for prime tasks.

Each of us has a unique set of energy rhythms and scheduled demands, and we should plan our lives accordingly. We consider these realities as we sketch out daily schedules and routines, but we should also take them into consideration regarding spiritual exercises. For instance, if one needs to be able to concentrate on reading the Bible for serious study, the morning hours may be most conducive. On the other hand, if one is reading the Bible for inspiration or memorization, reading the Bible in the evening may be profitable. Likewise, praying at the beginning of the day allows one to forethink and foresee the day, lifting its elements to God; evening times of prayer may be more conducive to personal reflection. So, depending on the nexus of one's obligations and the rhythms of one's day, setting prime time for prime tasks—and even changing things as needed to fit one's personal rhythms and the day's varying elements—works well.

Sometimes ways we structure our approaches are more ordered by the demands of the day. Parts of our schedules over which we have no control may provide their own "windows" into the life of devotion, and these can be approached opportunistically. An extra few minutes at lunch, or a brief time before other routines of the day get going or after they wind down—all of these become windows into deepening the life of the Spirit. So feel free to adjust and seize upon opportunities as they present themselves. And settle for small and apparently insignificant advances now and then, as well as larger ones, in seeking to deepen the life of the Spirit. Small pieces of thread do indeed a glorious tapestry weave.

Approach the life of devotion
with a sense of adventure!

Few things kill a venture like the bondage of obligation. Remember, the goal is not to set up a strategy; the goal is to go deep into the rivers of living water and to become a useful conduit of God's healing-redeeming work in the world. That's why the preparation is vital. So explore many ways to get there, not just a few. Be courageous! Bold! Risk failure, especially if you can learn something from it. If following a discipline falters, waste no time or energy with discouragement or lament; simply pick up where you left off and tune in again to God's presence and grace. That's the real goal, which our devotion aspires to prioritize, and yet it also is rooted in grace — not works.

Let your life become a living experiment in the way of the Spirit, and then be a steward of your discoveries. This is what is behind the spiritual discipline of keeping a journal. One records one's hopes, disappointments, discoveries, and reflections along the pathways of the spiritual adventure with Christ. One's learnings then become the stuff of experience to offer others, and in reflecting upon the walk of faith, ideals get ground up and tested in the crucible of everyday life. This is part of what changes a valued notion to a life-changing conviction.

We also seek to learn from others, and the devotional writings and journals of those who have gone on before us bear testimony to their ventures and the faithfulness of God. We do not travel this path alone! Here we can choose as our partners along the way the great devotional giants of the ages, and their learnings become our own as we read the devotional classics. But nothing speaks with quite as much clarity and authority as the personal testimony of God's leading and convicting work in our own lives. Obviously, the focus must ever be on God and what God is doing, and yet we discover a story to tell in the process. Personal testimony emphasizes not ourselves but the life of the Spirit into which we receive the remarkable invitation to be agents of primary research. The laboratory is our lives and the world around us, but the subject being engaged is the transforming love, power, and presence of God.

Read the Bible and steep yourself
in the devotional classics.

In reading the journals of Fox and Woolman, one sees the obvious: God's address through inspired Scripture was absolutely foundational to the personal formation of these spiritual giants. The same is true with Augustine, Luther, Calvin, Wesley, and so many others! What we find as we read the Bible is that the same Spirit who inspired the writing of the Scriptures also inspires us as we read them. At key junctures of our lives, memorized Bible passages become a source of genuine, divine guidance. And it is obvious that ideals formed through early reading of Scripture, as well as a pattern of life developed out of adherence to biblical themes, become the stuff of later direction and conviction. If Woolman and Fox had not steeped themselves early in their lives in the Scriptures, the history of the world would have indeed been different!

So, how do we get into the Bible? Good ways abound, but the most important thing to remember is simply to do it. *Read.* Whether spending a good deal of time focused on a narrow passage, or whether reading broadly (getting a sense of a larger unit), become engaged with the biblical text itself. I like to take a smaller unit, such as a chapter or a few paragraphs a day, and having read it thoughtfully to ask: "What does God want to say to me through this passage today?" Applications always come, and they often form the nuance and direction of spiritual impressions throughout the day.

Another approach is to read an entire book or a larger portion of a book in a single sitting. Time constraints may force this to be a weekly exercise rather than a daily one, but getting the sense of a writer's larger message and concern is always helpful. You find themes recurring and issues being addressed from more than one angle when you do this. Further, you get a better feel for the particular message of that part of the Bible, and you become sensitized to its distinctive voice within the larger whole. Getting the sense of the larger message of a biblical passage lends one greater interpretive authority than simply appreciating how it speaks to the individual. In looking at a smaller unit one can meaningfully say, "The Bible speaks to me..."; in looking at a larger portion one can more aptly say, "The Bible says...."

Take notes. Read a variety of translations and paraphrases. Learn Greek and Hebrew if you can; George Fox began learning biblical languages in his adulthood in order to get a fuller sense of the meaning of Scripture despite his concerns over the professionalization of theological study. Consider the context in which the original messages developed and were written, and learn as much as you can about ways the human authorship of the texts converged with the divine inspiration behind them. Learn to discern the heart of the biblical message over and above time-bound settings, in order to better apply the principles and patterns to our time-torn lives today. When that happens, application becomes exhilarating and God once again speaks in life-producing ways.

Get a balanced diet of prayer.

Prayer is not simply talking to God; it especially involves our listening to God. It is a response to the saving/revealing initiative of God, and therein lies its mystery. Jesus invites us to ask, and yet, even our requests reflect our sense of need—a sensitivity rooted in what God is doing. Sometimes our prayer lives are exciting and life changing; sometimes they seem dull and drab. Is God at fault? Probably not; the "dark night of the soul," to use the language of Saint John of the Cross, is often a reality for the Christian, calling us to press on in faith, but it is never without the hope of darkness-piercing dawn. In the life of prayer, getting a balanced diet may help.

The Bible describes several types of prayer, and yet all of them involve some aspect of the human-divine dialogue.

Words may be used if helpful to us, but God looks upon our hearts, and the communion that happens between ourselves and God is itself too beautiful for words. Paul speaks of "unceasing prayer" — that intercessory fluency empowered by the Holy Spirit — describing it as groanings beyond what words can express (Romans 8:26). Indeed, we are invited into an ongoing relationship with God within which we go through the day immersed in prayer, but also carrying on the business of the workaday world.

Develop a meaningful approach to the devotional life as a family or in community.

If you live within a family or a community, feel the freedom to develop meaningful corporate devotional experiences. Or, develop a small group or prayer partners in your life who you can support and from whom you also receive support. A family prayer time or a family Bible-reading time becomes a foundation for faith development in the formative lives of children, though our fractured schedules make it increasingly difficult. John Woolman's family used to read the Bible and other good books on Sunday afternoons as a part of their family's regular schedule, and it was during these times of reading and reflection that Woolman reports having developed a vision of what the people of God should be like — in his seventh year! Also, George Fox studied the Bible extensively, and William Penn declared that if the Scriptures were lost, Fox would have been able to reproduce them from memory. The day of "small things" one should not neglect. Upon these hidden foundations world-changing endeavors are established.

Prepare for the meeting for worship throughout the week.

The personal life of devotion deserves to be accompanied by regular participation in a community of worship, but participation should not be haphazard. During the week, preparing for the gathered meeting for worship should be performed conscientiously. Reflecting upon the previous meeting for worship and anticipating the next helps one with this venture, and preparing on Saturday evening for worship the next day quiets the mind and readies the heart for full participation. Developing an attitude of readiness for worship also allows one to make good use of any worship form, or the lack thereof. One of the greatest signs of spiritual maturity is the ability to enter into a meaningful worship experience, whatever the venue. In all the ways mentioned above, the life of personal devotion cultivated during the week enhances one's capacity to be involved in meaningful corporate worship as a participant, not merely a consumer. In so doing, we follow not only Jesus' example; we also become better prepared for following his leadership in the spontaneity of the present moment.

Set aside times for spiritual retreat and Sabbath reflection to reset your priorities and re-orient your life.

In addition to participation in weekly meetings for worship, spending time in solitude on a regular basis allows us to reflect on our lives and make adjustments as needed. This refreshes callings and clarifies priorities. Our many obligations in life become reordered as we offer them anew to God and allot concerns and commitments their proper place. On monthly, quarterly, and annual bases, time apart for prayerful reflection becomes a means of personal renewal and spiritual refreshment. Bible reading, prayer, and journaling are all valuable components of spiritual retreat—contributing, of course, to spiritual advance.

One exercise that can be helpful is writing a list of one's priorities in a column on the middle of a piece of paper: God, family, work, education, church, community, hobbies, projects, civic or social involvements, callings, and so forth. On the left side prioritize them from the highest priority to the lowest; on the other side rank-them in order according to the time and energy that you have put into each over the last two weeks or so. Then, note any discrepancies. If "family" is ranked second priority, for instance, but it ranks fifth in terms of recent time and energy invested, you have a decision to make. Either lower the priority or find a way to increase the time and energy invested. Circle any discrepancies that require adjustment and write in the margin how you, with divine assistance, will make changes to reconcile your perceived and actual priorities. Then make a new column with your reordered priorities and adjust your schedule and obligations if you can in order to live into the life you feel is pleasing to God. Our "ordered lives" confess the beauty of God's peace. With John Greenleaf Whittier:

> Dear Lord and Father of mankind,
> Forgive our foolish ways!
> Reclothe us in our rightful mind,
> In purer lives Thy service find,
> In deeper reverence, praise.
>
> In simple trust like theirs who heard
> Beside the Syrian sea
> The gracious calling of the Lord,
> Let us, like them, without a word
> Rise up and follow Thee.
>
> O Sabbath rest by Galilee!
> O calm of hills above,
> Where Jesus knelt to share with Thee
> The silence of eternity
> Interpreted by love!
>
> With that deep hush subduing all
> Our words and works that drown
> The tender whisper of Thy call,
> As noiseless let Thy blessing fall
> As fell Thy manna down.

Drop Thy still dews of quietness,
Till all our strivings cease;
Take from our souls the strain and stress,
And let our ordered lives confess
The beauty of Thy peace.

Breathe through the heats of our desire
Thy coolness and Thy balm;
Let sense be dumb, let flesh retire;
Speak through the earthquake, wind, and fire,
O still, small voice of calm!

In sum, the life of devotion is one of the great ventures of following Jesus, and it is essential to vital Christian faith and practice. Like daily-given manna in the wilderness, the bread which Jesus offers must be gathered daily, lest it spoil and cease to nourish. It is not the result of baptism; it *is* baptism — spiritual immersion in the life-changing Spirit of Christ. It is not the basis for communion; it *is* communion — spiritually lived out in unceasing prayer. And yet, as important as the life of devotion is, its value is facilitative, not ultimate. It deepens an intimate knowing of God and likewise being fully known, and *that* relationship is the priority of life itself!

The Lord's Prayer as a Transformative Pattern

Do you struggle with your prayer life? I do, and I think most people do as well. Jesus challenged his disciples in the garden: *Could you not wait with me [in prayer] one hour?* I have trouble with five minutes! If you're like me, upon entering a time of personal prayer you might find your mind wandering or yourself thinking about the demands of the day. Things to do, concerns about loved ones, pressures of the day, a twinge of guilt about an insensitive remark or a selfish deed — these distractions interrupt my prayer time; I imagine I'm not alone. But what if these distractions are actually the most pressing items we need to lift to God in prayer? Perhaps our inward "distractions" are the very things we need to offer back to God as a life-based outline of a prayer agenda.

I wonder if the lifting of these concerns to God might even fit a pattern of prayer that becomes a part of our spiritual growth and transformation. In my early adulthood I came across a pattern of morning and evening prayer, ordered around Ben Johnson's pamphlet "The Great Discovery"[2] and William Sangster's booklet *Teach Me to Pray*.[3] Since then, I have adapted it around the Lord's Prayer, which I'm coming to see as less of a text to be recited and more of a transformative pattern of prayer, helping us to go deeper into the life with God. Instead of 5 minutes being too long, I find that 15 or 20 minutes for prayer are often not enough. When God works in our lives, all things indeed become new!

The Bible describes several types of prayer, and yet all of them involve some aspect of what Abraham Heschel calls the human-divine dialogue. Words may be used if helpful to us, but God looks beyond our words to our hearts, and the communion that happens between ourselves and God is beyond what words can describe. The apostle Paul speaks of "unceasing prayer" (Ephesians 6:18 WNT)[4] as intercession empowered by the Holy Spirit. It is not simply we who pray, but the Spirit who prays through us (Romans 8:26-27). Indeed, we are invited into an intimate, ongoing relationship with

---

2. Ben Campbell Johnson, "The Great Discovery" (Decatur, GA: Lay Renewal Publications, 1965).

3. W. E. Sangster, *Teach Me to Pray* (Nashville, TN: Upper Room Books, 1959).

4. Richard Francis Weymouth, *Weymouth New Testament in Modern Speech* (Grand Rapids, MI: Kregel Publications, 1978).

God, within which we go through the day immersed in prayer, while at the same time carrying on the business of the workaday world. Developing a life of unceasing prayer, though, begins with immersing ourselves in the life of the Spirit, and such is helped by a discipline.

Really focusing on a particular kind of prayer as an intentional focus for a few intense moments helps us become immersed in praise, or thanksgiving, or dedication, or intercession, or petition, or prayer for protection, or meditation. It helps us develop sensitivity to the Spirit's leadings, and morning and evening patterns of prayer can be of great help in our spiritual development. In the Gospel of Luke we read that Jesus' disciples come to him and say, "Lord, teach us to pray" (Luke 11:1-4 NRSV). In the Gospel of Matthew (Matthew 6:1-15) we find Jesus gives his followers an approach to praying that poses a contrast to public performances and rote repetitions. Ironically, Christians sometimes use the Lord's Prayer exactly as that to which Jesus contrasts it. What Jesus provides them involves not a quotation to be recited as a vain repetition, but a pattern to be personally embraced, suggesting how we might approach God meaningfully in prayer. If you would like to try the following pattern based on the Lord's Prayer as a morning discipline of prayer, allow at least 10 or 15 minutes at the start of your day. Feel free to make adjustments as you need to; the goal is centering our lives on Christ.

A Morning Pattern of Prayer

Upon waking, turn your thought immediately to God. Either breathe a hymn of praise to God ("When morning gilds the skies my heart awaking cries: 'May Jesus Christ be praised!'") or muse over the psalmist's words, if helpful ("Bless the Lord, O my soul, and all that is within me, bless his holy name" — Psalm 103:1 NRSV). Find a place in which you can lift your heart authentically to God, and spend several minutes on each of the following themes. Brood over each until you are saturated with this particular aspect of prayer based upon the Lord's Prayer. Then, see what happens to the rest of your day. A balanced spiritual diet prepares us for living each day to its fullest. Nothing delivers us from a spiritual roller coaster like developing a grounded life of prayerful intimacy with God.

Our Father in heaven,
(Receiving the Divine Embrace)

Dwell on the wondrous fact that Jesus invites us to call God our "Father." This does not mean, of course, that God is not also like a Mother to us; indeed, God's nurturing and strengthening love embrace us in ways beyond our deservedness. Thank God for his goodness; his blessings are far beyond what we know. Elsewhere, Jesus calls God "*Abba*, Father" — a term similar to "Daddy" in English — the sort of endearing term a child would use to address a loving parent. Paul, in his writings, also uses this term. Come to God openly, as a child embraces the love of a divine father or mother, first thing in the morning. For of such is the kingdom of heaven

hallowed be your name.
(Adoration and Thanksgiving)

We *praise* God for who God is; we *thank* God for what God does. Let your awareness of God's majesty, goodness, and grace fill you with praise and adoration. Praise is not part of a transaction we produce; it is the only appropriate response to the authentic contemplation of God's glory. Jesus invites us to join the rest of creation in acknowledging the glory and holiness of the Creator. Praise God that God is the God God is, and let your life be filled with adoration and praise at the beginning of the day and otherwise. Also, thank God for what God has done. Our blessings are beyond what we can imagine; take the time to thank God now for family, friends, health,

life, grace. Ponder each blessing until you are filled with gratitude. Thanksgiving is an action that is never wasted! Let your
life be an ongoing chorus of blessing, thanksgiving, and praise
to God.

Your kingdom come.
(Dedication and Recommitment)

As well as lifelong vows to God, offer Christ your life anew —
totally and unreservedly — at the beginning of this day. Foresee and forethink the obligations of your day, and envision
God's presence with you throughout the day as you meet
those obligations. Respond to all things as though God were
working in them and through them; we live by faith, not by
sight. You can better face the already-scheduled events of the
day and even developments that are unforeseen through this
discipline of offering your life to God afresh. "Coincidences"
happen; openings emerge; things we'd planned go better, and
even surprises are more readily met by a life immersed in
prayer.

Your will be done, on earth as it is in heaven.
(Intercession and Uplifting the Needs of Others)

Lift also the needs of the world and the needs of others in
prayer, interceding on behalf of those persons and situations
for which God has given you a special concern. Keep a prayer
list, if you desire, or simply pray for those whom God brings
to your attention as you are mindful of such. Lift up family
and loved ones, friends and colleagues, projects and responsibilities, ministries and outreach opportunities — as partners in
furthering the active reign of God. The kingdom may indeed
come today, even in subtle ways, as people live in dynamic
responsiveness to his leadings and embody the way of the
kingdom in the world. Intercession is where the history of the
world is changed; it is there that the true business and work of
life are carried forth. Intercession is the spiritual work — the

heavy lifting we do as partners with Christ in the world, praying in his name *because* we have discerned and believe that it is according to his will.

Give us this day our daily bread.
(Petition and Uplifting Personal Needs)

Now lift to God your daily needs. God knows what we need even before we ask, and yet Jesus invites us to lift our needs to God in prayer. Amazing! The prayer of petition appropriately follows our adoration of God and our intercession for others, and yet an authentic sense of our need before God helps us be evermore keenly aware of our absolute dependence upon God for all things—even life itself. Lifting our needs to God, individually and corporately, also helps us release the particular ways we feel our needs should be met. In thanking our heavenly Father for provision ahead of time, desiring that our needs be addressed in God's ways and in God's timing, we assert our faith in what God is doing around us and within us.

And forgive us our debts,
as we also have forgiven our debtors.
(Confession and Forgiveness)

Receive now God's forgiveness and grace, availed through Christ Jesus, and extend such to others. He bore the sins of humanity on the cross, but acknowledging our sins and our need for grace leads us into the prayer for mercy. Christ died and rose for you and me. Those who extend mercy receive mercy, and our extending of forgiveness and grace deserves to be of the same character as that which we have received—or would like to receive. Turning to God with the conscious request for forgiveness further asserts our sense of humbled need before God. So, receive now the forgiveness and grace of God by *faith*, and extend forgiveness and grace to others by your *faithfulness*.

And do not bring us to the time of trial,
but rescue us from the evil one.

(Deliverance and Empowerment)

Trust God now for protection and empowerment. The prayer for deliverance from harm and ill asserts our trust in God's care and protection, both in ways we anticipate as well as in ways we cannot imagine. While trials bear within themselves potential for developing strength of character, Jesus also invites us to pray for protection and empowerment along life's way. Affirming the power and protection of God emboldens our courage and deepens our faith. As George Fox often declared, "The Power of the Lord is over all!" Abide now in the power of the resurrected Lord; it is available to all who believe.

For the kingdom and the power,
and the glory are yours forever.

(Centering and Meditation)

Close your time as you began it, with lifting praise to God and making your life a "living sacrifice" offered to his glory. Go through your day attending the business at hand, but also lifting prayers of adoration and intercession as you feel led. Attend the subtle promptings of the Spirit and live responsively to the divine will. This is the "centered" life—one that is attentive and responsive to the workings of Christ at the center of our lives. Give this day to God alone; dedicate it to the furthering of the way and work of the kingdom; extend the kingdom today by at least one life—*yours.*

Praying Throughout the Day

As you live your day, do so with spiritual sensitivity within the human-divine dialogue. Uplift those you meet with prayers of blessing and consolation; ask that God will also grant your being such to those around you. Allow the fruit of the Spirit ("love, joy, peace, patience, kindness, generosity, faithfulness, gentleness, and self-control"—Galatians 5:22-23 NRSV) to be evident in your life—the sweet-smelling fragrance that comes from knowing Christ (2 Corinthians 2:14 NRSV). Let your actions and your reactions further the love of God and the way of Christ among those you meet. Live in quick responsiveness to divine impressions and seek the Lord's guidance as you go about the tasks of your day. As Thomas Kelly says:

> There is a way of ordering our mental life on more than one level at once. On one level, we may be thinking, discussing, seeing, calculating, meeting all the demands of external affairs. But deep within, behind the scenes, at a profounder level, we may also be in prayer and adoration, song and worship and a gentle receptiveness to divine breathings.

> The secular world of today values and cultivates only the first level, assured that there is where the real business of mankind is done, and scorns, or smiles in tolerant amusement, at the cultivation of the second level. But in a deeply religious culture, men [and women] know that the deep level of prayer and of divine attendance is the most important thing in the world. It is at this deep level that the real business of life is determined.[5]

So, play a part today in God's changing the world through you and your living the day in prayerful responsiveness to divine leadings. Even your being moved to pray for those around you is not of your own design; it is granted by God as a means of drawing us into human-divine partnership. Allow also the Spirit to pray through you; such an experience, if it comes, may lend a feeling that prayer is less a matter of something we are doing and more a sense of a reality that is

---

5. Thomas Kelly, *A Testament of Devotion* (HarperOne, 1996), 9.

happening within and beyond ourselves. Why God would draw us into partnership in prayer is impossible to understand, other than its being a factor of deepest love and fellowship. That is why Jesus invites us to ask in his name and according to his will, assuring the granting of such requests. As we endeavor to discern a sense of God's will, authentic prayer affirms God's will into being. Such a prayer, because it furthers Christ's will, cannot go unanswered by the one who has planted it in our hearts.

Evening Prayer

Let your evening prayer develop into its own pattern as suits your needs. You might begin by reading John 17, the High-Priestly Prayer of Jesus, and allow a pattern to emerge from his exemplary prayer at the end of his ministry. Or, you might simply open your heart to God in a totally unstructured way and follow the lead of the Holy Spirit. The divine leading can indeed be trusted.

Whatever the case, you might close your day by reviewing the day and thanking God for the ways you discerned his workings and blessings throughout it. Thank God for his graciousness shown, and acknowledge also your continuing need for grace—a bit of posing here, or times you strayed from the way of Christ. Receive God's grace and also God's empowerment to do better. "This is what I am except I be changed into the likeness of Christ" becomes our attitude here. Authentic contrition is the basis for effective repentance. If there are particular concerns God brings your way, you may wish to add those to a prayer list. In addition to a list of concerns, you may also wish to keep a list of celebrations where God has indeed answered your prayers. Upon sleeping, turn your thoughts toward God as your head rests into the pillow. Give God your sleeping hours as well as your waking ones, and recall the words of the Lord on the cross: "Father, into your hands I commend my Spirit" (Luke 23:46 NRSV). Anticipate waking with praise on your heart and beginning the next day anew.

If we are not intentional about prayer, from the perspective of eternity we will wonder why we were such negligent partners in the human-divine discourse, which is what prayer is. The life immersed in prayer, however, indeed weaves a seamless tapestry; it is a life-changing adventure. Experiment and see what works for you. Modify your approach as you desire, keeping in mind that the following of a pattern is not the goal—abiding in Christ is the goal. To that end accept, abandon, or adapt particular plans in order that your life might indeed further the way and work of the kingdom in the world today. When that happens, prayer is not just something we do; it is something we become. Christ invites us into world-changing partnership, and when we enter into a life-transforming relationship, God's will is done on earth a bit more closely to the way it is in heaven. And for that, we join Jesus in saying, *Amen*—may it be so!

Embracing the Silence

Open worship is one of those traditions Friends embrace, but often we do so without much thought as to how to use the time meaningfully. While some unprogrammed Friends sometimes demur at too much expression, the tendency of some programmed Friends is to be uncomfortable with too much silence and to fill the "empty" space with words or other elements. After all, silence is a strange and foreign commodity within today's noisy society. Turning on the television or stereo becomes a semi-automatic reflex when one faces the shock of a quiet room. Seldom do we find ourselves able to

Earlier versions of "Embracing the Silence" were published in *Evangelical Friend* and *Quaker Life* in 1991.

pray for more than three or four minutes because of acute "spiritual attention deficit" disorders. We crave entertainment, while at the same time our lives are devoid of substance.

Tragically, we allow such shallowness to influence the meeting for worship until we find ourselves catering to the lowest common denominator among the least committed. We disallow reflective pauses between events in the service, worrying that "someone" might get bored. We ensure open worship is neither too long nor too embarrassingly silent, interrupting the divine word with our words of human origin. We fill the silence with background music to "assist" the distracted attender, and we always command a performance by the speaker, whether led by the Spirit to speak or not. We live in a world filled with words and noise, while at the same time we remain unreached by truth.

Ironically, at the very peak of the information age, the world suffers chronic malnutrition when it comes to being "fed" by the transforming Word of God. The modern myth that humans *can* live by bread alone is found to be naïve and falsely optimistic when tested by experience. People starve spiritually while the hunger goes ignored or misnamed. Well-meaning folk—both religious and secular—offer a plethora of words as though shells and husks had nutritive value. But the true need for the feeding of the human soul is the life-changing Word of God that comes to us as a divine gift, to be received and ingested through the embrace of faith. When this happens, all things become new. Life takes on new meaning and perspective, and the Word that spoke in the beginning of time becomes the creative and ordering source of all meaningful words today.

So what difference can open worship make, given our situation?

Several years ago during a meeting for worship, I gained a cluster of insights that continue to challenge and renew my life spiritually. Our family had worshiped at Glasgow Friends Meeting for more than half a year, and I found myself in a period of struggling with the discipline of silent worship. We had moved to Scotland for me to pursue doctoral work in New Testament studies at the University of Glasgow, and in doing so we transferred our membership to the local Friends meeting. By then I was more than aware of the cross-cultural differences between an American evangelical Friends pastor and the more understated manner of British unprogrammed Friends. This awareness caused me to be a little less extroverted with my spoken ministry out of sensitivity to the context, even though Friends had graciously expressed appreciation following the times I did feel led to speak. The result was that I had to face the silence straight on rather than filling it—a difficult assignment for one used to preaching and teaching at least three times a week!

This particular Sunday morning, after taking the first half hour to allow the "clutter" of my busied life to settle and to lift assorted concerns in prayer to God, I found my attention being drawn to the watershed marks of my spiritual life. I remembered the time when, as a fourteen-year-old at Canton First Friends Church, I asked Christ to forgive my sins and trusted him for the gift of salvation. I recalled many meaningful times of solitary prayer around a smoldering, summer-camp campfire. I also remembered being 16 years old and asking God to fill me with the Holy Spirit because my life had no empowerment. I saw that Christ needed to be my "lord," not just my savior. Then I recalled prayers for healing, some of which God had answered, and the lifting of other burdens to God, such as desire for direction for the future, concerns about relationships and loved ones, and awareness of the needs of others. What struck me about many of these times was that they seemed to have taken place during an "altar call" at the conclusion of a worship service, or during some other less-structured context of private prayer or corporate worship.

By now I was being drawn into a kind of Spirit-led "mental dialogue" in which questions demanding to be addressed seemed to emerge one after another. For instance: "What was it about an altar-call context that possessed such a life-changing capacity for you?" As I reflected on what really made the difference, I realized it wasn't primarily the music, or the speaker, or anything external. What truly made the difference was coming fully into the presence of God and seeing myself in the light of God's truth. God used human instruments, but mainly as a means of Christ's reaching the human soul. When this happens, our masks and façades fall away, and we face seeing ourselves as we really are. Truth is always convicting, and as we consider our true conditions, we find the Spirit of Truth faithful to convict us of sin and of righteousness (John 16:8-11). All of this heightens our dependence on God and causes us to draw more fully on his love, grace, and empowerment. We find ourselves changed women, men, and children, and spiritually better prepared to be Christ's agents of redemptive work in the world. Now that's transforming worship!

Another question followed: "Isn't that what is available to you (and every person present) right here, in this meeting for worship?" I had to agree, and in doing so began to view the silence differently. Rather than seeing it as a challenge to my undisciplined mind, I began to see it as a sacred place to meet with God. At once the value of open worship changed for me. Like the "holy ground" before the burning bush and the Pentecostal fire of the revival meeting, the silence had taken on sacred value. No longer was my focus on what somebody there, including myself, might share, but it had shifted to abiding in the present Christ—the true Word, from whom all inspired words come. Even the Scriptures come alive when the same Spirit who inspired their authorship also inspires their readership. Silence within the open meeting for worship creates what Parker Palmer describes as "the space in which the Living Word of God can be heard...and obeyed."[6]

A third set of questions followed: "If our goal is creating the space in which to encounter the living Christ, why reserve only the closing five or ten minutes for an altar call at the end of the service? Is not the singular priority of worship a transforming encounter with God? Why not do away with the 'preliminaries' and just have open worship as a corporate altar call?" I began to wonder what would happen if Friends from my own revivalist tradition would recover a sense of spiritual expectancy in worship. What would happen if people perceived the entire meeting for worship as a "corporate altar call" in which *all* came to lay their lives openly before the risen Lord, not just the few who might go forward at the end of a service? Who needs entertainment and festivities when people's lives are being genuinely touched by God?

Conversely, how many times is the Spirit of Christ stifled because there is no space for human-divine encounter to occur? I recalled with a bit of chagrin that in my own pastoral role, some of the most Spirit-filled meetings came as I yielded to a leading to lay aside the prepared message and to shift the focus to the present Christ as leader of open worship. People's needs were always met, and the needed message arose from within the gathered meeting. This caused me to reflect upon my own tradition and to explore how it might be restored to its original spiritual vitality. In doing so, several insights emerged:

1. The spiritually needy include far more than those who raise their hands during an appeal or who muster the courage to make their way forward at the end of a service. All seekers and finders need a regular setting in which to do real business with God and to bring their lives under the scrutiny of the convicting and comforting Spirit of Christ.

_____

6. Parker J. Palmer, *To know as We Are Known* (New York: HarperOne, 1993).

2. The focus of a meeting for worship should never be the speaker, with one's responsiveness determined by his or her fluency with humor or emotional appeal. Rather, it is the present Christ to whom all effective preachers and evangelists point, and only through a genuine encounter with Christ can a person be truly reached. Around this priority all forms of worship (and lack thereof) have their orbit. Their spiritual effectiveness is determined by the degree to which they serve the Center.

3. American evangelical Quakerism blossomed in the last couple of centuries when leaders and young people sought to revitalize staid meetings by introducing music and encouraging more spoken ministry. Yet vital worship is both expressive and impressive, and the same creativity that has encouraged expression over the last century or more can also be used to find fresh ways to recover the impressive aspect of worship.

4. Open worship has the potential of being the most sacramental of Christian experiences, as it is in this context that ongoing immersion in the Spirit—a deeply spiritual quality of communion—takes place. Likewise, transformative baptism involves inward rather than outward purification, and as such is a spiritual reality rather than a cultic one (*cultic* refers to a religious form in general). Within American revivalism the altar call had come to serve such sacramental functions as initiation, recommitment, and divine unction, but Jesus came to reveal that God's presence and grace are never limited to outward forms of human action. They are ever embraced and received by faith and expressed through faithfulness.

Jesus promised to be present wherever two or three are gathered in his name, not just when people use the "right words," raise their hands on cue, or perform rituals "properly." Christ came not to "narrow down" the options for how to experience God's presence and grace, but to reveal that

God can be presently at work in any setting, and that all human-made approaches to God are finally bankrupt in contrast to receiving God's gift of salvation mediated through Christ alone. After all, it is those who are willing to worship in Spirit and truth whom the Father seeks to draw into authentic and transformative worship.

In this age of words and more words, the world needs now, more than ever, the life-producing Word of God. Christ is truly present in the meeting for worship, seeking to comfort, convict, purify, and lead us into liberating truth. This kind of truth exposes our flaws, but at the same time it points the way forward, casting new light on society and our places within it. It is the stuff of which true revivals, conversions, and social reforms are made. It effects the healing of the individual and society. It calls us back to the ground and source of our being, and yet it propels us forward toward the imitation of Christ. It involves living into the belief that Christ is indeed present in the midst of those who gather in his name. This changes open worship from a bland form of passivity to an incendiary experience of spiritual renewal. Jesus said, "I came to bring fire to the earth" (Luke 12:49 NRSV), and that is what we encounter when we open our lives fully to him in the gathered meeting for worship.

On Worshiping in Spirit and in Truth

In the second decade of the Quaker movement, laws were passed designed to set back the movement's headway because it was so contagious and threatening to official religion in England. These anti-Quaker laws made it illegal for people to meet together without permission (permission that was, of course, denied to Friends) and for nonconformists to live within five miles of incorporated towns. The laws also required oaths to the king and the use of Anglican worship rites, barring anyone from civic leadership who did not participate in Anglican liturgy or sacraments. As a result, thousands of Friends were imprisoned for their faith, and many suffered and died in prison. So many Quakers were thrown into Lancaster Castle around this time that the best way to reach members of the local Friends meeting was to write to the prison! At stake was the belief that Jesus was right when he declared that authentic worship is in Spirit and in truth, and that God is actively seeking to encounter any and all who seek to worship authentically.

Misconceptions about authentic worship, however, are not confined to seventeenth-century England. All too easily people nowadays confuse worship with a performance for which we are an audience. We might comment on the style of music or the effectiveness of a speaker, as though such factors determine our ability to worship God, but in reality they have little to do with authentic worship. The central factor in the quality of worship is *our* willingness to be drawn into the loving presence of God—receiving God's love and expressing our love for God—regardless of the venue. Worship also involves our attributing worth (worth-ship) to God; the ways in which we respond to the truth of who God is and stories of what God has done factors into worship's fullness. As participants in worship, *we* are the performers, not detached observers. Therefore, the lead question for evaluating the vitality of a meeting for worship is not "How did others do?" but "How did *we* do?" in our response to God's working in and through the words, music, silence—or lack thereof. A lively participant in worship is never bored.

It is also a misconception to see worship as a solitary venture only, when it thrives most within community. Christ has promised to grace us as we gather in his name, and his presence is especially powerful within the gathered meeting. The burning ember smolders and eventually goes out if it is left to itself, but as logs on a fire radiate heat together, so gathering together for worship warms and encourages believers. Coming to worship expectantly, prepared to do business with God or to be used by God if led, makes one's corporate experience of worship a meaningful engagement. Private worship is important, but gathering with the people of God on a regular basis is foundational to any authentic experience of worship.

Another fallacy is the notion that worship involves a transaction with God. Too easily we construe the meaningful activities of worship as "things we do in order to get something from God." Expressions or movements may assist the worshiper, but they never impress God, nor are they ever what God requires. God looks upon the heart, and those who come to God in simple trust find God and are likewise found by God. Praise and adoration are therefore meaningful in worship, not as something to be done in order to obtain a spiritual feeling or even a gift from God. Rather, they are merely the authentic responses of the heart to our glimpses of some aspect of the truth about God. As nature itself praises God simply through its being, the one species created in the image of God lifts its praise by a choice—by acknowledging who God is in responsive adoration. One cannot say anything truer about God than by employing the language of praise and adoration. In that sense, praise is a loving response to God's character and loving initiative toward humanity. It is offered spontaneously and freely rather than offered for what one might expect in return. Our lives do change as we worship—for the better—and yet this comes as a grace rather than a recompense.

A final misconception about worship is that we can improve it by what we add to it. Oftentimes, we get the notion that doing worship in the right way or in the right place will improve the worship experience. Indeed, aesthetic factors come into play here, and we may enjoy some forms and expressions of worship more than others. But where the measure is authenticity and genuineness, simplicity of form may be more conducive to the real thing, and openness to the Spirit of God is far more important a factor than special places or surroundings. Neither to Jerusalem nor the Samaritan mountain is the authentic worship of God confined. Rather, the condition of the heart makes all the difference, and those who are open to human-divine encounter are the sort of people God actively seeks to draw into transforming worship.

Such convictions, however, may lead to an obverse problem — that of seeing silence or formlessness as a new sort of form. What George Fox and early Friends sought to recover in their attentive waiting upon the Lord together in silence was the very fountain of living water that Jesus promised would flow out of the innermost beings of those on whom he poured out the Spirit (John 7:37-38). They sought to drink from the headwaters of the streams of inspiration rather than from their collected pools, and Fox even envisioned the prophets of old being carried along by the Holy Spirit in empowered meetings for worship as they wrote the Scriptures, imbued with inspired authority (2 Peter 1:21). What the Scriptures teach, and what believers have experienced, is that Christ is indeed alive and wanting to lead the church. When we open ourselves to the life-changing power and presence of Christ in the gathered meeting for worship, Pentecost is changed from a biblical memory to a contemporary experience.

There is no substitute for the outpouring of the Holy Spirit in the gathered meeting for worship, and the Lord's day of visitation may be closer than we think. Rather than being something for which we reach up to bring down, however,

Christ has promised to be present wherever we gather in his name. The question is not whether the present Christ will visit our meetings for worship; he is here, even closer than our mouths and hearts. The question is whether we will open ourselves to his saving/revealing initiative and respond in faith and praise to his secret power and presence among and within us. When this happens, we experience the sort of authentic and spiritual worship Jesus talked about, and God's endeavor to draw his beloved into this life-changing reality is actualized!

According to the Richmond Declaration of Faith (1887): "Worship is the adoring response of the heart and mind to the influence of the Spirit of God. It stands neither in forms nor in the formal disuse of forms; it may be without words as well as with them, but it must be in spirit and in truth (John 4:24)."

"The ministers of Christ were not idle. They
gathered sticks together, and kindled a fire, and left
it burning." (**Robert Fowler,** Captain of *The Woodhouse,* 1657)

"And in a word, we are for a holy, spiritual, pure, and
living ministry actuated and influenced by the Spirit
of God in every step. By the Spirit they are called,
qualified, and ordered as ministers, and without it
they cease to be ministers of Christ." (**Robert Barclay,** 1678)

"Dear Friends, keep all your meetings in the authority,
wisdom and power of Truth and the unity of the
blessed Spirit. Let your conduct and conversation
be such as become the Gospel of Christ. Exercise
yourselves to have a conscience void of offense toward
God and toward all people. Be steadfast and faithful
in your allegiance and service to your Lord, and the
God of peace be with you." (**Elders of Balby,** Yorkshire, 1656)

"The outward modes of worship are various, but wherever
men [and women] are true ministers of Jesus Christ
it is from the operation of his spirit upon their hearts,
first purifying them and thus giving them a feeling
sense of the conditions of others." (**John Woolman,**1720-1742)

"We have often wondered whether there is anything Quakers today
can say as one. After much struggle we have discovered that we
can proclaim this: there is a living God at the centre of all, who
is available to each of us as a Present Teacher at the very heart
of our lives. We seek as people of God to be worthy vessels to
deliver the Lord's transforming word, to be prophets of joy who
know from experience and can testify to the world, as George Fox
did, 'that the Lord God is at work in this thick night.' Our priority
is to be receptive and responsive to the life-giving Word of God,
whether it comes through the written word—the Scriptures,
the Incarnate Word—Jesus Christ, the Corporate Word—as
discerned by the gathered meeting, or the Inward Word of
God in our hearts which is available to each of us who seek
the Truth." (The World Gathering of Young Friends Epistle, 1985)

Part IV

Ministry
and
Christian Service

Apostolic Ministry

When George Fox declared that "being bred at Oxford or Cambridge" does not make a person a minister of the gospel, he challenged the priesthood of his day for limiting the supply of God's mercy to official dispensers of grace. He opposed those who made careers out of citing "chapter and verse" but did not show in their lives evidences of scriptural living. He confronted the ways the institutional church of his day had become self-serving, co-opting its ministers, and he sought to recover nothing less than the heart of apostolic Christianity.

Ironically, many who should have been most pleased with reforms that Quakers sought to effect were most threatened by the Quaker message. Until Parliament passed the Act of Toleration in 1689, the Church and government of England opposed Friends and other dissenting groups in the name of "apostolic succession" and authority. They effectively banned Quakers from societal leadership and even institutions of higher learning because admission and good standing required oaths of loyalty and participation in Anglican worship.

All of this was legitimated by claims to "apostolic succession," and ironically, the son of an admiral in the British Navy, young William Penn, was expelled from Oxford in 1662 for failing to comply with enforced religious requirements.

So what does it mean to follow in the succession of the apostles? Does it mean Christian leaders must be biological descendants of Peter, John, or Paul? Of course not, although James, the brother of Jesus, was the first head of the Jerusalem Church. Following in the line of the apostles has nothing to do with dynasties. Every generation must avail itself to God anew. Pentecost comes not by schedules of calendars but by seasons of divine visitation, and such wonders happen when God's advances and human responsiveness converge.

Another misconception is that the succession of the apostles is organizational. Of course, many assume the office of "apostle" follows a structural designation within the institutional church. Granted, there are important historical reasons as to why the church has adopted institutional structures, and leadership responsibilities must always be clarified. But the mistake is to limit understandings of apostolic ministry to the confines of organizational structures. Jesus did not come to replace one organization with another. He came to expand access to God for all who believe, and to extend the invitation of apostolic partnership to all who would join him in the important work of reaching the world with the good news message of God's transforming love. "As the Father has sent me," declares Jesus, "so I send you" (John 20:21 NRSV).

Believe it or not, the apostle Paul faced challenges as to whether he was a legitimate apostle. He was challenged in 2 Corinthians 11 by "super apostles" claiming he was neither charismatic enough, nor connected enough, nor solicitous enough to be considered an apostolic leader as they themselves claimed to be. In Paul's response, however, he clarified the meaning of apostolic ministry. To be an apostle is to have

encountered Christ transformingly and to have been sent by
him in service to the world (Galatians 1:1-12). This is also what
Friends believe.

George Fox and the early Quakers, in seeking to recover
the essence of apostolic ministry, lived by several standards
rooted in both Scripture and experience. They sought to embody the ministries of the apostles, and only time will tell how
close they came in that aspiration. And yet, the relevance of
any endeavor relates to the difference it makes for the present.
So, consider these testimonies and see if they are outdated or
just as relevant as they were centuries ago.

Apostolic ministry, according to Friends

...is based on transforming encounter with Jesus.

There is no substitute for encountering Christ personally and
offering one's life wholly, completely, unreservedly to God.
Education is important, but it can never replace the human-
divine relationship, which is one of faith. The apostle Paul
encountered the risen Christ on the road to Damascus; George
Fox caught his vision of "a great people to be gathered" on
Pendle Hill. For some of us, encountering Christ happens a bit
more subtly, but engaging the risen Lord has been and will
always be the central basis of apostolic ministry.

...involves being sent by Christ on a mission with a purpose.

Apostolic ministry is never the sort of thing that emerges from
mere human initiative or ingenuity. It always involves being
sent by God. Sometimes God sends us by means of a concern
that wells up from within. Sometimes God works through
others. "Would you be willing to help with...?" someone asks.
This involves a calling—a vocation. Jesus called his disciples
first to be with him, and then he sent them out on ministry
assignments (Mark 3:13-15). When George Fox was asked

where he came from, he responded with a great sense of humor: "I came from the Lord." And, the "Valiant Sixty," comprising mostly young adults who were captivated by Fox's three-hour sermon at Firbank Fell in 1652, spread all over the civilized world with the good news of Christ. The love of Christ constrains us, and that love becomes the energizer of apostolic mission.

...is characterized as partnership with Jesus.

Jesus says you are my "friends" on two accounts: first, because of doing whatever Jesus instructs us; and second, because the Father's work is made known to us. The best way to understand John 15:14-15, the passage from which this testimony comes, is to see it as an invitation to apostolic partnership with Jesus, an invitation Jesus extends to every believer. We become sent, just as he was sent by God (John 20:21-23), and we are invited to be one, even as he and the Father are one (John 17:11, 21). A daunting prospect! But the issue here is not metaphysics; rather, it is a matter of missional connectedness. When we open ourselves to the work God would be doing through us, we feel a double sense of urgency: God is the source of all concern and empowerment, and yet for some reason, God chooses to use frail folks like you and me in furthering his work. This is a humbling realization, yet it is the core of effective Christian service.

...is "released," not remunerated.

Tom Mullen used to say with a half-smile that Friends do not believe in a paid ministry, only a "partially paid" ministry. No one ever got rich off of serving in ministry among Friends. Then again, Friends have correctly sided with the spirit of Paul and the other apostles, who followed Jesus in the teaching: "Freely you have received, therefore, freely give." Christian ministry is not something ministers charge for, as though it were a subcontracted specialty. To treat it that way is to make a mockery of the cross and to misrepresent the gospel. Also, too easily a "hireling" flees when there is danger rather than being willing to offer true and sacrificial care for the sheep after the manner of Jesus (John 10:11-12). On the other hand, ministry takes time, energy, and resources, and Friends have described a person's receiving this type of support as "being released" for ministry. In that sense, the minister is not "paid" to do acts of service; rather, she or he is released from having to be tied down to a place of employment and so can be free to serve as the flock of Christ needs. Being released for ministry need not, and perhaps should not, involve dependence on a salary. It may come through retirement, or through being able to live simply on less, or from being able to work gainfully in another occupation, liberating one's time to be used in God's service to others. The apostle Paul made tents, and he found ways to minister extensively without requiring remuneration, while also welcoming support. The question for all is how to become released in order to carry out the work God has for each of us to do.

...is at times "recorded" as public ministry ordained by God.

Humans do not ordain others for Christian service; only God does. And yet, Friends do believe in recording that God has gifted some for special public ministries, and this implies that God has ordained their service. Any call to serve is also a call to prepare, which will involve academic, practical, and spiritual preparation for ministry. The recording process therefore considers evidence of one's calling as attested publicly in real life, seeking also to ensure preparation in fulfilling one's vocation. Has one been called by God, and does one's ministry show evidence of divine giftedness and calling? These are the questions that lead to the assessment that one has indeed been called and ordained by God for Christian service. When Friends have identified members as showing these evidences, the status of "recorded minister" is sometimes granted by means of a recording process. While benefits may be modest, when Friends recognize one's calling and ministry as being used by God meaningfully, this can be empowering, and the community affirms that the workings of God in the past will be indicators of further ministry to come.

...is empowered by the Holy Spirit.

The most important preparation for ministry is the spiritual preparation that happens when the Holy Spirit transforms a person's life. Just as the gift of grace is received through faith, the gift of empowerment is received by trusting in the work of the Holy Spirit in our lives. Jesus reminded his disciples to trust the Spirit's leadings when they were brought up before trials and tribunals, because the Holy Spirit would give them the words needed at the right time. Speaking a prophetic word from the Lord comes as the one who is sent also becomes open to being a mouthpiece for God. The goal, thus, is to be faithful to the convicting work of the Spirit in one's life, and to uphold the truth above all else — because the truth indeed liberates!

Many Christians would agree that apostolic ministry is an essential part of Christian ministry, but the question is how we enter effectively into that reality. Does it hinge upon an office-based history of human succession, or is it founded upon the inspired character of transforming encounter with the risen Lord? Scripture points clearly to the latter, and so does Christian experience throughout history.

These are but a few characteristics of apostolic ministry as Friends have understood it. While apostolic ministry seeks to recover the best of the days of the apostles, the focus is not retrospective. The goal is to be open to what the risen Christ would do through each of us in the present—children, men, and women. As we become open to what God might do in us and through us, we offer all of our gifts and abilities to his service. And yet, apostolic ministry hinges upon one's primary ability—our *avail*-ability—and when we offer that to God, the days of the apostles are here again!

Members of the Crew

As a high school senior seeking direction as to what to do with my life, I received this insight from my pastor, Joe Roher: "Paul, your vocation is already decided for you." "Good!" I thought. "Will it be a law career or teaching art?" He went on: "You are called to be a follower of Jesus Christ. Now, the way you invest your energies and earn your subsistence should be the means by which you are the most effective disciple possible."

That made sense to me, and a couple of months later my understanding grew further. As a counselor at Quaker Canyon Camp's "Adventure Camp," preparing to make a presentation for fifth and sixth graders on the possibility of God's call to missions, God actually spoke to me: "Are you asking those kids to do something you're not willing to do yourself?" "No," I responded, "I just need to know the calling to ministry is *your* doing, not my agenda." The Lord then confirmed this calling to me by means of several Scripture passages (especially Romans 10:15), and directly I decided to attend Malone College (now University) and pursue studies in psychology and Christian ministries.

Several years later, as a young pastor and seminarian at Earlham School of Religion, my mentor Elton Trueblood challenged me, saying, "If you are a Christian, you are a minister.

An earlier version of "Members of the Crew" was published in *Evangelical Friend* in 1993.

A non-ministering Christian is a contradiction of terms." And, "The church of Jesus Christ is a ship that carries no passengers; for *all* are members of the crew." And again, "*Laity* is a bad word. Don't use it! The New Testament church knew of no distinction between laity and clergy....The goal of the pastor is not to be 'the' minister, but to be about the task of helping others identify and carry out their own ministries. That is the ministry of multiplication, and perhaps the most crucial ministry of all." Not a bad definition of "vocational" ministry!

"Vocation" comes from the Latin word *vocare*, "to call," and as we consider our callings in life, the organizing interest has less to do with what one might gain from life and more to do with what one is called to contribute. Over the last three or four decades, many of the greatest strides toward Christian renewal have been taken as a result of churches recovering that Reformation and Quaker ideal: The priesthood and ministry of Christ extends to *all* believers, not just a handful. The question is not *if* a committed Christian will minister, but *how*.

Genuine ministry can happen, though, through a variety of venues. A working definition might be: "Ministry involves identifying human needs and meeting them, energized and empowered by the transforming love of Jesus Christ." The vocational question is thus: "By what avenue has God called you and me to further his loving reign and redemptive work in the world?" Vocation implies a calling; vocational ministry is something we do through our occupations, not just in addition to them.

The authentic follower of Christ works neither for self nor gain, but to serve the needs of others as Christ's hands and feet in the world. This may be one of the best means of Christian witness we can imagine. Work becomes one's context and means of ministry, and not surprisingly, genuine service always succeeds. When people serve others effectively and genuinely, that becomes a compelling witness.

Who would not want to return to a business or service that went above and beyond expectation, motivated by a calling to serve others sacrificially and well? So it is also with Christian ministry.

From the beginning of the movement, as Friends developed traveling ministries, they often combined preaching and inspirational ministries with other venues of service. It is therefore no surprise that as revivalist ministers sought to further the healing of war-torn North America after the Civil War, Friends were among the traveling preachers and ministers God used in that ministry. As preaching circuits yielded fruit in terms of people coming to the Lord, interests in traveling ministers spending more time in a region led to the pastoral system within the Quaker movement. Within that system, however, the conviction remains that while public ministry may be a special calling for some, God calls all to minister in the common ventures of life; we gather to worship, and we scatter to serve.

In 1657, a second group of Quaker "Publishers of Truth" felt called to travel to America in order to share the everlasting gospel. Some of them had been there before, and were even banned from Boston by Puritans seeking religious freedom for themselves while unwilling to extend it to others. Having convinced Robert Fowler, the captain of a small ship named *The Woodhouse*, to avail his ship to the cause, they were forced to wait for favorable winds at Portsmouth before heading across the Atlantic. While waiting, though, they held meetings for worship on the boat, inviting local Friends to join them and inspiring their ministries with the fellowship. About this apparent delay in their mission, Fowler wrote in his journal: "The ministers of Christ were not idle, but went forth and gathered sticks and kindled a fire and left it burning."

So how do we deal with the opportunities of life, as well as its apparent setbacks? Indeed, every turn of events becomes an opportunity for ministry if we will but open our lives to what Christ would be doing in us and through us. In this consumerist age, Christians may wrongly ask, "What am I getting out of this church?" The vocational question is, "How am I best able to serve—within this church and beyond it— connecting human needs with the transforming love of Jesus Christ?" And, such an inquiry may lead to one of the most important journeys of all: the transition from being a passenger to becoming a member of the crew.

The Prepared Messenger

Every calling to serve is also a calling to prepare. As such, this involves preparation for a particular meeting for worship in which one is expected or may feel led to speak, but it also involves lifelong preparation in service to lifelong callings. Between these two realities, Friends have emphasized the prepared messenger over a prepared message. Of course, prepared messages are valuable, as the Spirit leads during preparation, but minding the leadings of the Spirit also in the delivery of a message is central to effective gospel ministry. And, to do so requires one to be a prepared messenger.

Regarding particular meetings for preaching and teaching, spoken ministry is not the same as delivering a speech. At times, a preacher may read or recite a message—even effectively—but this is not the same as speaking directly to the needs of a community based on an immediate sense of leading and personal engagement with those present. Eye-to-eye contact enables one to speak *to* others, not just *at* them. The ministries of Jesus and the apostles do not come across as delivered speeches, prepared scripts, or the enacting of memorized roles. Rather, apostolic ministry seems to have been occasioned by an explosive combination of the sensing of human needs and the prepared messenger's willingness to minister faithfully as led and empowered by the Holy Spirit.

Therefore, the messenger prepares for worship by praying earnestly about a message to be shared from the Lord. As a message emerges, and as one reads, reflects, and gets the content into a manageable form, the burden grows and takes on definition. What began as a general spiritual concern for the meeting grows into a timely message for the group, informed by readings from Scripture and other inspiring writings, until the message is clear in the heart and language of the messenger. Sometimes an object lesson from personal experience or a graphic illustration captures the imagination and becomes a vehicle for conveying the truth of the kingdom with gripping clarity. Whatever the case, the minister prepares personally and spiritually in order to be especially sensitive to the Spirit's leadings before and during the gathered meeting for worship.

Likewise, the spiritual elders of the community, whether serving on a committee as such or otherwise, endeavor also to prepare for worship ahead of time, bathing the meeting in prayer. In that sense, each one comes to worship expectantly, ready to be used of God as a mouthpiece of the divine Word if called upon to speak. However, this is not the same as coming to worship intending to speak or planning to deliver an address. The leadings of the Holy Spirit can be trusted, and there is no need to pre-empt them ahead of time. On the other hand, the Spirit may indeed lead during the week in ways that are serviceable to be shared during the meeting for worship, so preparation indeed finds its direct delivery from time to time.

One of the variables, of course, is whether the meeting is programmed or unprogrammed, or some combination of both. Where one is charged with bringing a message, focused preparation during the week is essential. Reading and studying a biblical text within its literary context, considering how it was used to address concerns in its original settings, allows parallels to be applied within later ones. Indeed, where a pastor is charged with regular preaching and teaching, providing spiritual nourishment for a congregation in sustained ways, he or she must give first priority to discerning the Lord's leading for the group and planning one's preparation accordingly. One pastor I know used to take the several weeks during the summer in studied retreat, laying out a year's worth of biblical messages to prepare. Whether working with a sermon series based on a theme or progressing through a set of texts, such an approach provides a sustained and sustaining means of nurturing a flock, which is what the spiritual gift of *pastor-teacher* implies. After all, Christ can lead before a meeting for worship as well as during one.

Despite one's labor before a meeting, however, the spiritually sensitive minister must be prepared to lay a message down if led to do so. If the Holy Spirit is leading the prepared messenger to set aside the prepared message, the Spirit will surely provide the divine word to be delivered in ways timely and fitting. The message from the Lord will still come, but perhaps through others, and powerfully so. In addition to preparing well as preachers and teachers, we must continually prioritize adequate time to respond to the Spirit's leadings if our meetings are going to be imbued with their deserved vitality. The same may be the case with leading discussion groups, Sunday school, or Bible studies. Creating the space for the Spirit to lead may be the most important service one can provide.

Where the meeting is an unprogrammed meeting, preparation is still important, but the expectation of ministry is more broadly distributed. Within such settings, single individuals are not normally charged with bringing a regular message, but all are called to prepare as though the Lord's message may come through them. An elder may read a Scripture text or a query from *Faith and Practice* to focus the reflections of the gathering at the beginning of the meeting, but even with such a prompting, the focus is on the Lord's message for the group. As a result, the word that Christ might be bringing to the community is furthered by the sharing of each, as every person who shares aspires to be used of the Lord — connecting one's impressions of a leading to what has been contributed before. As a result, one may be led to speak along the lines that had not been considered ahead of time, simply as a leading, adding to the divine word that has been emerging from others within the gathered meeting.

Likewise, where there is a time of open worship after a sermon in a programmed meeting for worship, the interest of those who feel led to speak is often most edifying as it continues the word of the Lord that has already been spoken. Of course, other Spirit-led concerns may also be shared, but within the gathered meeting — where the Spirit of Christ truly gathers his flock around a particular concern — vocal ministry will continue to fill out the larger set of concerns for people to consider in spiritual depth. In fact, responses following a message in open worship may be the most important time of the gathering. People's responses to the word of the Lord are most apparent during this time. Whether a holy silence falls upon the group, or whether people feel called to put faith or prayer into practice, or whether one or more people extend or amplify the divine message through their contributions, it is there that spiritual communion is most profound and most palpably encountered. And the preparation and participatory engagement of those present that makes it possible.

Preparing for worship and ministry on a weekly basis is one thing, but how does one prepare for a lifelong calling to public ministry? While Friends have long emphasized spiritual preparation for ministry as being central to effective service, ironically the testimony of Fox that one need not be "bred at Oxford or Cambridge" to become a minister of the gospel has been misunderstood to imply that our leaders need not be well educated or prepared for ministry in systematic and sustained ways. Nothing could be further from the truth! Jesus prepared thirty years to minister for three. Fox had memorized the Scriptures by heart as a youth and had a good understanding of church history. Further, if it were not for Robert Barclay's first-rate theological education, it is certain the Quaker movement would never have had the extensive appeal it did. He originally wrote *An Apology for the True Christian Divinity* in Latin to convince the European intelligentsia of the relationship with Christ as being the core of Christian vitality, not a provincial endeavor to safeguard the Quaker witness as a local movement confined to northwest England. Barclay thereby sought to have an impact reaching around the world.

As a movement endeavoring to change the world, we must devote ourselves to providing all aspiring leaders with the support they need, not only recognizing their callings, but also assisting them in preparing systematically and rigorously for exercising those callings. On the one hand, learning by doing is one of the best approaches to getting good at something. Jesus sent out his followers in ministry groups of twos, even before they had received sustained education. In addition to spending time with the Master, Jesus' followers also gave themselves to the learning of Scripture, and most of the writings of the New Testament reflect the development of Christian "schools" and discipleship-training endeavors. Certainly the Gospels of Matthew and John reflect such communities of learning within the early church.

Following that pattern, getting involved in ministry profitably happens early on, with gospel teams and social outreach being carried out among all ages—from our young people to our senior citizens. Likewise, sustained approaches to learning are also a must—from solid Bible-study programs for children and youth, to adult-learning programs, to ministry internships, to first-rate college and graduate studies in Bible, theology, and ministry. Of course, shouldering the cost of such investments deserves to be shared by all who believe in and will benefit from them. Many a Christian leader discovers too late in the throes of pastoral or missionary service the limitations of one's educational preparation. Therefore, young people need to pursue basic levels of education *before* assuming weighty responsibilities. The pursuit of continuing education over the course of one's entire life is also valuable. An ongoing interest in learning is essential for young and old alike!

Again, to be called to serve is also to be called to prepare for that service, and more than a dozen Quaker colleges and half a dozen Quaker Bible schools and graduate programs in ministry have been established for the rigorous preparation of those who are called to serve in terms of Christian ministry—full-time or otherwise. Effective pastoral work is so demanding precisely because it involves knowledge and skill in many fields, not just one. Therefore, preparing others for ministry is one of the most important callings in life. Indeed, affording those with leadership potential meaningful opportunities to learn and prepare for ministry will multiply one's impact in exponential ways, and such ventures always deserve sacrificial support.

When God spoke to the world via his Word, he sent neither a text nor a curriculum—he sent a person. Likewise, what the world needs now is not merely a prepared message, but prepared messengers, equipped and empowered to further the word of the Lord faithfully and effectively the world over. The goal of public ministry is not for a human speaker to be heard, or even enjoyed; rather, the goal is for the life-giving word of Christ to be heard and received effectively in faith. Therefore, the messenger does all she or he can to imbue the meeting with prayer, and also to prepare herself or himself to attend and discern the Spirit's leadings before and during the meeting for worship. Lifelong preparation for service continues as a calling for every serious disciple of Jesus; after all, the word "disciple" means *learner*. Prepared sermons? They are important at times, and people are well served by a message diligently and prayerfully prepared. But far more effective is the prepared messenger who, if led to lay the sermon aside or even to stray from a point or two, is in touch with the leadings of the Holy Spirit at work in the meeting, seeking to revive, quicken, and heal. When a messenger responds faithfully to the Spirit's guidance, not only is the word of the Lord delivered, but the life-giving Word of God is encountered.

The Universal Ministry

"Greetings, favored one! The Lord is with you!" were the words the angel Gabriel announced to Mary (Luke 1:28 NRSV). After regrouping from the shock of it, and after receiving support from her cousin, Elizabeth, Mary exclaimed, "My

---

An earlier version of "The Universal Ministry" was published in *Evangelical Friend* in 1991.

soul magnifies [and amplifies] the Lord, and my spirit rejoices in God my Savior!" (Luke 1:46-47 NRSV). What if young Mary would have said *no* to God's desire to use her in his unfolding plan of salvation? Or what if Joseph or Elizabeth would have dissuaded her from following the Lord's leading in her life? Heaven and earth would be the less for it, and the divine mission of Jesus would have been thwarted. Few ministries are absolutely gender-specific, but this was certainly one of them.

To extend the parallel, I wonder if Friends are as supportive as we should be of women who have sensed a divine calling to serve among us in ministry. If not, the entire body of Christ will suffer impoverishment. Obviously, the calling of Mary was a unique one, but there may be some nurturing, pastoral, instructional, or organizational needs within the church to which God calls specific people—not in spite of their being women, but even because of it. All of this comes to mind in the light of knowing several talented and well-trained women who had a clear calling to pastoral ministry but did not find places to serve. I don't know why that was the case, but it raises the query: If God calls women to serve, why don't some of today's churches?

That's a question I've wondered about for some time now. I remember hearing stories about my grandparents, Scott and Grace Clark, both recorded ministers who responded faithfully to God's call to ministry, and I wonder what the Lord is doing among his people today. Grandpa served as president of Friends Bible College (now Barclay College) for its first 18 years and as pastor of several Quaker churches, but Grandma, also a recorded Friends minister, was every bit as active in ministry. In hearing my uncle Roy Clark describe her call to ministry, I learned Grandma used to say God called her to ministry because others turned their backs on a call to minister to the youth of their community. Sometimes a lively concern for the need at hand becomes a source of God's working in our lives, and we must be open to however God moves.

Some of the first things my grandmother would do when her family entered a new community were to start a jail ministry, prayer meetings, Bible studies, a youth group, and a WCTU (Women's Christian Temperance Union) chapter. A few years ago, a pastor in Eastern Region told me with a twinkle in his eye: "Your grandmother sent me to jail." He then described how Grandma would organize six or more carloads of adults and young people and take them to the county jail for Bible studies. These early experiences in ministry played a formative role in his own calling into the pastoral service. Indeed, early experiences of ministry bear within themselves the seeds of vocation if we can remain open to the Lord's workings in and through them. And, the WCTU movement, for all its limitations, sought to address radically the social problems related to alcohol abuse in the American home: worsened economic hardship, spouse and child abuse, and wage-earning instability. In that sense, the temperance movement addressed some of the same concerns that recent feminists have addressed, and in some ways more effectively.

Grandma was also quite an evangelist herself, and she and Grandpa held extensive outreach campaigns. Recently, my mother showed me a poster from the 1940s advertising "Grace Coppock Clark, Quaker Evangelist" as a speaker featured at revival meetings held in Colorado Springs. Both my mother, Lucy Anderson, and sister, Marva Hoopes, have been recorded as Friends ministers in Evangelical Friends Church—Eastern Region, so Grandma's legacy continues, and God persists in working through all who are open to his callings. All of this makes me appreciate how Friends continue to be faithful to the Lord's leadings in terms of openness to young and old, and men and women, using fully their gifts for ministry nowadays.

Indeed, we have a strong heritage to honor as well as future callings to fulfill. At the beginning of the Friends movement, Margaret Fell came to be known as the "Mother of early Quakerism" — opening her home at Swarthmore Hall and helping institute the Kendal Fund in support of early Quaker traveling ministries. Mary Fisher felt led to witness to the sultan of Turkey and traveled to the heart of the Ottoman Empire to witness to gospel truth. Mary Dyer and four other Quakers were hanged on Boston Commons for preaching the gospel despite being sent away and warned accordingly. Elizabeth Fry was instrumental in effecting prison reform in England. Indeed, the prophecy of Joel 2:28-32 was fulfilled at Pentecost and ever since, as God's Spirit is poured out on the young and the old — male and female — on the day of the Lord's visitation (Acts 2:18).

During the first part of the twentieth century women enjoyed a greater freedom to live out their spiritual callings in terms of pastoral leadership within the church. In Kansas (now Mid-America) Yearly Meeting, for instance, more than one quarter of the active, recorded ministers were women during the first half of the century. Since World War II, however, the percentage of women ministers active in virtually all North American yearly meetings declined fourfold or more. Some explain this phenomenon as the result of a compensatory adjustment after a popular war. In exchange for the brave and valued service of American (male) soldiers during the early 1940s, jobs were "created" for the returning men, and the roles of women who had filled the labor needs in factories and the rest of society were reassigned back into the home in the late 1940s and 1950s. Unfortunately, we still have a ways to go in recovering from this adjustment.

Before this time, Quaker girls as well as boys were encouraged to consider God's calling them to full-time Christian ministry, and many responded faithfully. The question we ought to be praying about now is how to be proper stewards of the spiritual giftedness and callings of all members of Christ's body, as opposed to appropriately stewarding only half of them. Still more importantly: Are we following the Holy Spirit's leadership fully in the ways we encourage, identify, and utilize forthcoming leadership, including young and old, male and female — all who feel called to Christian ministry? With the coming of Christ, the universal ministry is now a reality, as Jesus filled his followers (plural) with the Holy Spirit, commissioned them as apostles sent from the Father, and imbued them with authority to be forgivers of sins (John 20:21-23).

The way we look at the gospel therefore makes all the difference when it comes to ministry. Many well-meaning Christians interpret the New Testament wrongly, seeing it as delimiting gender roles when it actually does the opposite. Jesus came to show us the true picture of how God works, and the Gospels of John and Luke in particular present him as honoring women as his disciples as well as men. God is not a respecter of persons, races, or genders. All have access to him through Christ, and all are expected to respond to his invitation into loving relationship. Granted, Paul appealed for church order in ways patriarchal, and he had particular concerns about some female converts to Christianity in Corinth. Nonetheless, his inclusive example and teaching elsewhere — ministering alongside Priscilla and declaring that in Christ there is "no longer Jew or Greek, there is no longer slave or free, there is no longer male and female " (Galatians 3:28 NRSV) — marks a new day with the new covenant.

Thank goodness Mary said *yes* to the Holy Spirit! May we also be given the grace to respond as faithfully, and to prepare the way so that all who feel genuinely called to serve may do the same.

A Motion of Love

Effective Christian ministry is inspired in its empowerment, inclusive in its scope, and compassionate in its character. In 1996 our family drove across the country to Philadelphia, where I did research on Henry Cadbury in the Quaker Collection at Haverford and served as a visiting scholar at Pendle Hill. During that visit, Chuck Fager took us to the archives of the Friends Historical Collection at Swarthmore College, where we were allowed to view the original handwritten copy of John Woolman's *Journal*. As we looked at this historic manuscript, two things impressed me. First, Woolman had done significant editing, adding words or phrases and deleting others. It reminded me of the adage Jack Willcuts often shared: "There's no such thing as good writing, only good *re*writing." A second insight follows. In the first sentence, Woolman inserted "of love" into the first sentence, so that it reads: "I have often felt a motion *of love* to leave some hints of my experience of the Goodness of God, and now, in the thirty-sixth year of my age, I begin this work." Indeed, Woolman was moved by God in his ministry and in his writing, but he describes that motion as compassionate in its character. It was not simply an abstract sense of feeling moved; it was a "motion" of divine love.

In that sense, authentic ministry flows directly out of authentic worship. We gather for worship; we scatter to serve. In apprehending the love and truth of God, we cannot but be drawn into praise and adoration — worshiping in Spirit and in truth. In seeing the truth about ourselves, in the light of God's presence and love, we are transformed and entrusted with a sense of mission; authentic vocation flows directly from seeking to be stewards of transformative encounters with the Divine. And, seeing the truth about others—getting a "feeling sense" of their condition (using Woolman's language)—forms the basis for loving ministry and social concern. When we see people as they really are, we cannot help but be drawn into serving their needs, energized and compelled by the love of Christ within. Knowing the truth is always liberating (John 8:32), and God's love and truth go hand in hand.

In Woolman's case, he became personally troubled over slavery as he was charged with writing a bill of sale for a slave. He said that seeing that woman as a person—"one of my fellow creatures"—moved him to believe that slavery as an institution was wrong. While he wrote the bill of sale then, Woolman subsequently refused to do so, recording that "I was so afflicted in my mind, that I said before my master and the Friend that I believed slave-keeping to be a practice inconsistent with the Christian religion." Woolman therefore began speaking against it, and he spent the remaining 30 years of his life seeking to convince Friends in America and Britain to abandon slavery. In 1759, when he spoke to and prayed with the Native Americans in Wehaloosing, Pennsylvania, chief Papunehang declared, "I love to feel where the words come from." Woolman's own description of that meeting for worship was that the "current of love" had run strong, and he was not alone in that perception. Woolman died in 1772 on his mission to London Yearly Meeting, after speaking to this anti-slavery concern at their annual sessions.

One more story comes to mind. In the early nineteenth century, the French Quaker minister Stephen Grellet felt moved to preach to a group of woodcutters deep in the Pennsylvania forest. He was faithful to his leading, but when he arrived, the camp was deserted. Rather than leave, he acted upon his leading and declared the gospel of Christ in the mess hall, although no one was in sight. Six years later, as he crossed a bridge in London, a man approached him and declared, "I have found you at last!" Confused, Grellet said he must have mistaken him for someone else, but the man went on to share that he was in the woods the day that Grellet preached, having returned to the abandoned campsite to retrieve his lever. Upon hearing a voice, he listened and felt as if an arrow had pierced his heart. The man was convicted about the immorality in his life, and when he later found a Bible to read, he discovered the way to salvation, changing his life. The man continued, saying he had then become an evangelist, and by that time had reached no fewer than a thousand souls for Christ. Ever since that day in the woods, he had been searching for that preacher and wanted to express his gratitude for the preacher's faithfulness.

We never know what may come of a motion of love or a quiet leading; most often we only glimpse the results of faith from a distance. The love of Christ constrains us, though, and we can trust the leadings of the Spirit beyond what we can imagine. As we abide in Christ and his love abides in us, we become sensitized to the conditions of those around us, ready to be touched by motions of love and the liberating power of truth. Indeed, the faithfulness of such people as Woolman and Grellet inspire our responsiveness to leadings we may encounter, and the words credited to Grellet ring true in our own experience as they did in his: "I expect to pass through this world but once. Any good, therefore, that I can do or any kindness I can show to any fellow creature, let me do it now. Let me not defer or neglect it, for I shall not pass this way again."[1]

---

1. Walter Williams, *The Rich Heritage of Quakerism* (Newberg, OR: Barclay Press, 1987), 149. (cited in a somewhat different form)

"I think I can reverently say that I have much doubt
whether since the Lord by His grace brought me into
the faith of His dear Son, I have ever broken bread
or drunk wine, even in the ordinary course of life,
without devout remembrance of, and some devout
feeling regarding the broken body and the blood-
shedding of my dear Lord and Saviour." **(Stephen Grellet**, 1860)

"We reverently believe that, as there is one Lord
and one faith, so there is, under the Christian
dispensation, but one baptism, (Ephesians 4:4, 5)
even that whereby all believers are baptized in the
one Spirit into the one body. (1 Corinthians 12:13)
This is not an outward baptism with water, but a
spiritual experience; not the putting away of the filth of
the flesh, (1 Peter 3:21) but that inward work which,
by transforming the heart and settling the soul upon
Christ, brings forth the answer of a good conscience
towards God, but the resurrection of Jesus Christ,
in the experience of His love and power, as the
risen and ascended Savior." **(The Richmond Declaration**, 1887)

"The presence of Christ with His church is
not designed to be by symbol or representation,
but in the real communication of His own Spirit.
'I will pray the Father and He shall give you another
Comforter, who shall abide with you forever,'
(John 14:16) convincing of sin, testifying of Jesus,
taking of the things of Christ, this blessed Comforter
communicates to the believer and to the church, in a
gracious, abiding manifestation, the REAL PRESENCE
of the Lord. As the great remembrancer, through
whom the promise is fulfilled, He needs no ritual or
priestly intervention in bringing to the experience
of the true commemoration and communion.
'Behold,' saith the risen Redeemer, 'I stand at
the door and knock. If any man hear my voice and
open the door, I will come in and sup with him and he
with me.' (Revelation 3:20)" **(The Richmond Declaration**, 1887)

Part V

Sacraments and Sacramental Living

======================================

A Theology of Presence

One particular Sunday morning after delivering a sermon on prayer, a woman shared with me about several unfortunate turns of events in her life. "I tried God," she said. "It didn't work."

Job's comforters came to "help" him in his distress saying something like, "Okay, Job, what have you done now? There must be some reason why all this is happening to you. Fess up, repent, and God will make it better."

First-century Jews longed for a Messiah who would come and rid the land of the Roman menace—setting up the center of God's rule (and therefore Jewish power) once more in Jerusalem. But Jesus was killed as a common criminal at the hand of the Romans. He was rejected by his own, and those who followed him were ridiculed by the masses and persecuted by rulers. Was this *success*?

An earlier version of "A Theology of Presence" was published in *Evangelical Friend* in 1993.

SACRAMENTS AND SACRAMENTAL LIVING | 1 13

All too easily we fall into the trap of assuming God's main interest is to make things good for us. On one hand, that's true. God loves us as our heavenly parent and desires nothing but the best for our lives. God is the giver of all good gifts and is also the ground and source of our very being. If God were not, we would not be. On the other hand, the ways God blesses us begin and end with a new relationship. He offers us his presence, and out of that reality all true blessings flow.

When we begin to take that seriously — when we begin to look at life through the eyes of faith — all things indeed become new. Rather than being conformed to the pressures and measures of the world, we become transformed by the renewing of our understandings and minds, discerning, then, what is good, acceptable, and perfect (Romans 12:2). We begin to develop a "theology of presence." In many ways, the healing and saving power of God's presence is the main theme of the Scriptures:

- In the beginning, humans walked with God in the garden — enjoying the communion of God's presence — but because of sin they (and we) became alienated from God and strangers to God's presence.

- God's promise to Moses before the burning bush was "I will be with you" in his commission to tell Pharaoh to release the Israelites. God's presence provided strength and empowerment.

- God's presence guided the Israelites through the wilderness, as a fire by night and a cloud by day. Centuries later, the ark of the covenant "enhoused" the presence of God in their midst. God's presence produced guidance, empowerment, and deliverance.

- The ideal government, God's righteous light shining from Zion, eventually became the aspiration of the Jewish nation — that holy mountain of the Lord where the lion would lie down with the lamb and swords would be beaten into plowshares. All would thrive under their own vine and fig tree (a Jewish cliché for prosperity), and none would make them afraid. God's presence made society fair, peaceful, prosperous.

- Eventually, the same God who spoke through the prophets and the Scriptures spoke to us though his Son. The Word became flesh and dwelt among us. He brought healing to those he touched and the saving reality of God's presence to those who believed.

- Through Jesus, the saving/healing power of God became accessible to the world in ways never experienced before. Through him the Holy Spirit is poured out beyond measure. God's presence is now available to all.

Indeed, the great sacramental mystery of the Bible is that God, in Christ, is reconciling to world to himself, and also reconciling divided peoples to one another. As the Latin word *sacramentum* is used to translate the Greek word *mystērion* in the New Testament, never is God's "mystery" (and thus, "sacrament") associated with a cultic rite or form. It is always connected with reconciling work of Christ; it is a gift of indwelling presence—"Christ in you, the hope of glory" (Colossians 1:27).

Jesus promised his sacramental presence wherever two or three are gathered in his name, promising also to be with his followers in their discipling ministries unto the end of the age (Matthew 18:18-20; 28:20).

As well as being scriptural, a theology of presence also impacts our daily lives. It is all too easy to think of God as our divine problem solver who helps us figure out life's mysteries and delivers us into success. Yes, God does all those things, and certainly crises and challenges drive us toward a deeper dependence on God, but the sequence is a paradoxical one. Only by releasing our sense of need to God and resting in

God's presence do we find our true needs addressed. At times our true needs differ from our perceived needs, and God sometimes changes our awareness of our true conditions.

We may think we need that item, that measure, or that esteem from those particular people, when actually what we need most is relationship. All our needs reflect our deepest need: the need for God. To "try God," as though God were a prescription to remedy life's problems, is to miss who God is. God is a person, and persons require relationships. Once we become immersed in the loving presence of God, we do indeed find healing and provision, but sometimes they come in ways we had not imagined. False dilemmas become exposed, and new alternatives emerge. God does miracles around us, and sometimes within us. To commit our needs to him is to commit every part of our lives to him, encompassing all we invest, receive, and experience.

Religious folks also like to be "right," and God often becomes a co-opted ally in fielding this temptation. Is the would-be Christian predictor of the events and sequence for the end times all that different from the soothsayers and false prophets the Old Testament warns against? It puzzles me to note the ease with which those who build great and glorious schemes based on "literal" Bible prophecies overlook the literal counsel that those who speak presumptuously in the name of the Lord (and whose predictions do not come true) should be put to death (Deuteronomy 18:19-22). A convenient oversight, of course!

In defiance of the biblical answer-men of Job's day, God overturned the conclusions of religious wisdom. Calamity is not necessarily the result of human sin; sometimes even the righteous suffer, and tragedy is finally inexplicable. Assessing blame rarely does any redemptive good. The sovereign God stands above all attempts to find answers from the heavens, and the turning point of the entire book of Job is found in verses 5 and 6 of chapter 42. Here Job declares that "seeing"

God begins the way forward. We may think that what we need is the right answer, but God meets our deeper need and provides us with his presence. To see and to encounter God is enough; this happens by faith.

In Jesus we see a radically new portrayal of success. Success is not a factor of "winning" or doing better than the competition. It has to do with faithfulness to God's truth and living out of a life-changing relationship with God. In the light of God's presence, successes, failures, and other "impostors" may be viewed more adequately — from the perspective of eternity. In the incarnation, God's world-changing presence was also manifested in human form. God conveyed his redemptive and healing love in person form, as persons have a greater capacity to convey than do inanimate rites and objects.

When we come to see the world through the eyes of faith, new possibilities emerge. We begin to see traces of God's presence and subtle workings in the world in ways we'd rarely imagined. Through Scripture, church history, the gathered meeting, and our times of prayer, the living Word of God addresses us and makes all things new. Not only do we see new possibilities for God's saving and healing presence to work redemptively in the world, but God begins to use us as active means of that work. Not only do we develop a theology of presence, that's what we become!

On the Character of Sacramentality

What makes something sacramental? For the apostle Paul, the "mystery" (the word behind the term "sacrament" in Latin) of the ages is that God is reconciling the world through the

An earlier version of "On the Character of Sacramentality" was published in *Evangelical Friend* in 1992.

epoch-changing work of Christ. The classic answer, going back to Saint Augustine, is that a sacrament is an outward and visible sign of an inward and spiritual reality. During the middle ages, the church embraced as many as thirty sacraments, but Peter Lombard reduced them to the seven that are still a part of the Catholic faith. Luther and the Reformers reduced the number to two, as water baptism and the eucharist are the two most closely connected to New Testament practices. But what is it that really makes something sacramental? Or, put otherwise, what is the character of sacramentality?

Unfortunately, Quakers have at times been shallow in their treatments of the issue. They easily stress what they *don't* do and miss the whole point of a very beautiful and meaningful testimony — one the world still needs desperately to hear!

It's also true that many who may have found the outward use of sacraments meaningful in other traditions often miss the community experience of a water baptism or the outward celebration of the Lord's Supper, and Friends might not serve them well in their explanations of spiritual approaches to these realities. Further, sacramental restlessness among Friends may be a sign that the local church leadership has not thought enough about how people experience the real presence of Christ in the gathered meeting for worship, how every worship meeting should create the space for "communing" with the risen Lord, how the Holy Spirit can fill and transform the individual with Pentecostal fire, how God can miraculously reach the world and the heart of sacramentality — how the Divine is made accessible.

One can appreciate the sentiment of those who advocate "liberty" regarding outward sacramental practices, especially if the local congregation has been sacramentally dormant. But this does not mean Friends' positive testimony about the sacraments has become obsolete; it has simply been unexplored.

Liberty of ignorance, however, is not the same as liberty of conscience.

So just what is the positive Quaker testimony on the sacraments? In a nutshell, God looks on the heart and the one who believes in him fully receives him fully. Outward ways of expressing ourselves to God and before others *never* determine God's divine action toward us. Authentic trust alone is the sole condition for receiving God's saving grace and sanctifying power.

The right words? God knows our thoughts even before we speak. The right postures? God sees through to the very core of our beings. The ritually, politically, or socially "correct" way? God is above all of these. He loves us and sent his Son to die that we might live into the newness of life. Forgiveness of sins, forsaking the world, spiritual immersion, divine empowerment — we receive all of these through faith in Jesus Christ alone. The only true outward evidence of saving faith is the changed and changing lives of those who abide in Christ and are immersed in his Spirit. Friends believe this is what Christ came to bring, and that no religious group or method regulates the divine dispensing of grace. Because God's grace is all sufficient, nothing else is required.

Of course, objections come from Christians wanting to be faithful to their understandings of the Bible, and this is always a worthy concern. Clearly, some early Christians practiced adapted forms of Jewish water purification rites and held thanksgiving (eucharistic) meals of remembrance, although there was a great deal of diversity regarding the ways they did so. A closer look at the New Testament, though, helps us consider how early Christian sacramentality developed, starting with Jesus.

Two of the first things you notice about Jesus are that he dined with tax gatherers and sinners, and that he pronounced woes upon the scribes and Pharisees. But these stories grow shamefully "tame" to our ears. Table fellowship in those days was a statement of acceptance and solidarity between parties. They believed that God was present in a special way in the breaking and sharing of bread. Jews were not allowed to eat with Gentiles or with those who were ceremonially unclean. This would taint them too. Further, to be deemed a "sinner" was in effect to become a social outcast. It was the price of not living up to the ceremonial and legalistic letter of Moses' law. Social anthropologists call these "purity laws," and all cultures have them. They prescribe what members of a society must do in order to become legalistically acceptable and ceremonially pure.

What Jesus did in that context was absolutely astounding! By claiming to be God's envoy, and by dining with the "impure" and rejecting the "pure," he declared to the world that God's saving presence is never confined to outward ways of doing it right. Jesus' teachings and deeds in all four Gospels make this motif abundantly clear. God looks on the heart, and those who trust humbly and authentically in him will be saved. Conversely, those who trust in their human-made attempts to obtain God's saving favor will always founder.

The cleansing of the temple marks another radical demonstration by Jesus, but this time it is one of judgment rather than inclusion. The division of the masses into two camps, the pure and the impure, motivated even the poor to try to go beyond their means. They were forced to purchase more expensive "legal" sacrificial animals and had to pay a markup rate to exchange Roman currency for Jewish coins. In some cases, this reduced the standard of living significantly for the already poor, and it even made it impossible for the people of the land to feel they had any access to God's grace. Nearly the entire lower class of people was deemed "sinners" — people who did not, and could not, attain ritual purity, and who were considered outside the grace of God. But Jesus declared them to be acceptable in God's eyes, and he drove out of the temple those who made a profitable trade of religious systems of purification.

This was no mere rejection, however, of one religious system to be replaced by another. Jesus came to reveal the absolute bankruptcy of all human effort and instrumentality, as far as receiving God's grace is concerned. This applied to first-century Jewish religion, and it applies to us today. On these matters, Paul's teaching of salvation by grace through faith alone was right on (Romans 1:16-17). He understood Jesus' teaching and mission perfectly well from a theological standpoint.

So what about the "ordinances"? If believing in God though Christ was enough, why did Jesus ordain water baptism and the eucharist? Or, did he *really*? When we look at baptism and communion in the New Testament, the following becomes clear.

Regarding Baptism

1. The central exhortation associated with baptism and the eucharist, when mentioned together by Jesus, was embracing the cross — not participating in a cultic rite. For instance, when Jesus asked James and John, "Are you able to drink the cup that I drink, or be baptized with the baptism that I am baptized with? " (Mark 10:38 NRSV), he was not quizzing them on their willingness to get ritualistic. Clearly, he was referring to their willingness to suffer, and even to die, for their Lord.

2. Literally, all the times the New Testament mentions together the baptisms of John and Jesus (Matthew 3:11; Mark 1:8; Luke 3:16; John 1:26-33; Acts 1:5; Acts 11:16), baptism with fire and

the Holy Spirit as Christ's baptism is clearly prioritized over John's water baptism. John's baptism prefigured the baptism of Jesus, but the latter is always emphasized over the former. It always seems odd that those who insist on the literality of water baptism fail to make the same interpretive move when it comes to baptism by fire, the baptism of Jesus, to which John's baptism pointed. The spiritual immersion always supersedes the hydraulic one in the Bible, and this is what all Christians ought to affirm.

3. Sometimes baptism with water failed to be accompanied by the baptism of the Holy Spirit, and this was a problem. When Philip baptized Samaritans (Acts 8:12-17), some of them failed to receive the Holy Spirit until Peter and John came along and laid their hands on them. Apparently in the middle first century some of the followers of Apollos knew the baptism of John but did not know there was a Holy Spirit. Paul ran into some of these people at Ephesus (Acts 19:1-6), and after he explained John's baptism of repentance was to help people believe in Jesus, Paul baptized them in Jesus' name. He then laid his hands on them, and they were filled with the Holy Spirit. Water in these cases was clearly insufficient. One must be born of the Spirit (John 3:5b), or one's life is not transformed. Water cleanses the skin, but only the Holy Spirit can purify the soul.

4. Perhaps because of this event, or simply because of the sometimes-unclear relationship between spiritual realities and outward practices, jealous divisions arose also in the 50s of the first century AD, between those who had been baptized by different Christian leaders. Some claimed, "I am of Paul;" some claimed, "I am of Apollos;" some claimed, "I am of Cephas;" and some said, "I am of Christ." All of this partisan dissension makes Paul declare, "I thank God that I baptized none of you except Crispus and Gaius!" (1 Corinthians 1:14 NRSV). Obviously, Paul is not saying he was glad not to have

evangelized or not to have made disciples more than he did. The problem was that Corinthian believers had begun to pride themselves in who had performed their outward baptisms, assuming it made a difference in terms of spiritual effect. This made Paul want to give up water baptism altogether. "For Christ did not send me to baptize but to proclaim the gospel," he declared (1 Corinthians 1:17 NRSV).

In the light of how the sacraments have come to be seen as nearly magical effecters of the divine presence within some sectors of Christianity, Paul surely would have sided with the Quaker testimony as to the spiritual character of sacramental reality. Just as he opposed the use of circumcision as a sign for new believers, he would certainly have opposed the association of other Jewish forms as a requisite of saving faith. Circumcision must have been meaningful to many, and it too had a biblical precedent, but the new covenant through Christ Jesus has done away with all rites—Jewish and otherwise. It is received by faith alone.

5. Apparently, a generation or so later, some were even claiming Jesus performed water baptisms, but John 4:2 sets the historical record straight: "It was not Jesus himself but his disciples who baptized" (NRSV). While water baptism became the standard for symbolizing the new Christian's rejection of the world and decision to follow Christ, it did not originate with Jesus' practice or teaching, according to John. The baptism of John actually took root as an alternative to Jewish ritual cleansings, which may have washed the outside but did nothing on the inside. Water baptism became an institutional Christian rite of induction by the second century, but first-century Christian leaders are shown debating the character and use of this evolving Jewish-Christian practice with considerable disagreement. Spiritual baptism, on the other hand, is always the New Testament priority, and such is the essential baptism emphasized by Paul (Ephesians 4:4-6).

Regarding Communion

1. Just as John emphasizes that Jesus himself never baptized, John completely omits any institution of the eucharist at the last supper. This is extremely odd if the writer of John was indeed an eyewitness! If he were there, and if instituting a meal of remembrance was Jesus' primary purpose at the meal, why did he not pick up on something so important and so obvious? The only "ordinance" in John 13 is the command to love and serve one another, as Jesus exemplified in washing his disciples' feet. The more pressing question is not why did John leave the words of the institution out, but why did Mark (who is followed by Matthew and Luke) include them?

2. Mark clearly identifies the last supper with the Passover Feast of Unleavened Bread (Mark 14:12-25) and connects the redemption offered through Jesus with the ultimate focus of something like the Jewish seder meal. As they broke the bread of thanksgiving, recalling deliverance in the wilderness, the biblical text portrays Jesus as having said something like, "The true deliverance symbolized by the breaking and eating of this matza bread is not the exodus of long ago, but my body — broken for you."

Likewise, as they raised the cup of redemption — recalling the blood of the lambs smeared on the door posts of Hebrew houses in Egypt, causing the spirit of death to "pass over" those households — Jesus is portrayed as having said something like, "The true redemption symbolized by the Paschal lamb is really the blood of my covenant which will be shed for you on the cross." All of this suggests less that Jesus was trying to "ordain" a new ritual and more that he was intently seeking to transform existing customs by showing how they ultimately prefigure his sacrifice on the cross. He was not emphasizing the need for the Jewish Passover meal in order for people to have their sins remitted, nor was he superseding a

Jewish rite with a "Christian" one. Rather, he redirected the imagery of the Passover meal to his own sacrifice—given for all time—which supplants the need for animal sacrifices and the meals that follow them. The Passover points to the cross! This is the point of Mark's rendition of the Last Supper, and it reflects the emerging view of mainstream Jewish/Christian communities around the middle of the first century AD.

3. In 1 Corinthians 11, however, we see a distinct move from a fellowship meal to a ritual meal within the Corinthian church. This is the first historical evidence of such a transition, but notice it does not happen until more than two decades after the departure of Jesus. In chapter 10 Paul describes believers coming together for fellowship meals—perhaps like the kind that Jesus ate with sinners and tax gatherers, and certainly with his disciples at many times. This is the sort of Christian table fellowship described by Luke in Acts 2:42-47 and 4:32-37. Early believers experienced spiritual communion as they broke bread together and celebrated table fellowship in real-meal settings.

What becomes clear, however, is that some Corinthian participants had begun abusing table fellowship (1 Corinthians 11:17-22). They were inconsiderate of one another, cutting in line, eating more than their share while others went hungry, getting drunk. Far worse than most Quaker potlucks I've attended! In response to this, Paul replaces the fellowship meal with a symbolic meal, calling it the "Lord's Supper" and citing the words of the institution (vv. 23-26). From then on (the mid 50s), if anyone is hungry, that person should eat at home (v. 34). Luke clearly adopts Paul's language in his presentation of the Lord's Supper, which by then had evolved from a fellowship meal into a formal one. Was there ever a Christian ritual and symbolic meal before that time? There may have been, but we simply have no evidence of such, and inferences along those lines may suggest a projecting of later customs onto the early church more than reflecting accurate historicity. The formalization was a later evolution, not the earliest Christian practice.

4. Between the writing of Mark and the writing of Luke (a decade or two later), we see a further transition from the contents of the cup (Jesus' blood) to the cup itself (Mark 14:24; Luke 22:20). "This cup that is poured out for you is the new covenant in my blood," reads Luke's rendition (NRSV), which is very similar to Paul's. Whatever the reason for it, we clearly see an evolution from Mark's attaching christological significance to the Jewish Passover meal to Luke's and Paul's rendering of the Lord's Supper as a "Christian" ceremony. This, nonetheless, is far from representing historically an ordained ritual by Jesus himself. In that sense, partaking in a symbolic meal was probably never an ordinance of the Lord. It emerged in his memory, but it cannot be said to represent his cultic desire for believers.

5. The instruction to eat Jesus' flesh and drink his blood in John 6:53-58 does not refer to the indispensability of the eucharist for salvation. This becomes clear in the light of verse 51. This "bread" offered by the Son of Man is his flesh, given for the life of the world; to ingest it is to be willing to go to the cross with one's Lord. If one hopes to be raised with Christ on the last day, one must be willing to suffer and die with him in the present. In that sense, ingesting the flesh and blood of Jesus bore the same meaning as sharing his cup and being immersed in his baptism in Mark 10:38-39. They stand as symbolic images of Christian martyrdom—literally, not as ordinances toward ritualism proper. To deny one's Lord in the world is to be denied by him before the Father in heaven. This is why refusing to eat the flesh and drink the blood of the Son of Man is to forfeit divine life. The death-producing danger in John 6:53 was always believers being assimilated into the

world — not the lack of assimilating bread and juice into one's stomach.

The point of all this is to show that the same Jesus who revealed — with eschatological finality — that God's grace is not limited to participation in Jewish ritual means of purity did not ordain new, Christian ritual practices to take their place. The more I learn about the New Testament, the more Quaker I become. The Friends testimony that true sacramentality hinges totally upon the inward authenticity of the believer's faith, not an outward means of ritual purity, is precisely what Jesus came to reveal. It wasn't until the second or third Christian generations that ritual means, as opposed to inward trust and corporate fellowship meals and meetings, were devised, emerging within the middle-to-late first-century church not without struggle or controversy. Jesus came not only to tell the world how to encounter God; he came to *be* that communication and locus of encounter.

So what is the character of sacramentality? When God wanted to communicate his saving love to the world with finality, he didn't send us a ritual, a book, a song, or even a good sermon. He sent his only begotten Son: God's Word made flesh (John 1:14). The ultimate sacrament — the greatest physical conveyance of spiritual reality *ever* — is therefore the incarnation! Why? An incarnate form of sacramental revelation has far more capacity to convey God's saving love and grace than do inanimate objects and rites. In fact, objects and rites have no power to convey the divine, and they even detract from it.[1] This is why God forbade the Israelites to erect graven images. Many may have felt they were "helpful," but the God of Moses and the God revealed in Jesus declares otherwise.

---

1. Alan Kolp, "Friends, Sacraments, and Sacramental Living,"
   Quaker Religious Thought #57 (1984).

The All-Sufficiency of Christ

All of this comes down to the most important issue—the all-sufficiency of Christ. If Jesus Christ is all-sufficient, to add anything to Christ is to diminish Christ. God requires nothing other than a believing response to his saving initiative—which Jesus Christ was and is. To say we need something else is to refuse the Incarnation and to deny the cross of Jesus. To recommend Jesus plus anything else is to declare that his sacrifice is less than enough.

As well as diminishing the all-sufficiency of Christ, the symbolization of inward faith by any measure other than Christlike love diminishes one's faith. It puts the emphasis on creaturely activity rather than the work of the Creator. It misconstrues the human-divine relationship as one of instrumentality (we do "x" in order to get "y" from God) rather than trust. It makes gods of our puny measures rather than giving us the opportunity to respond to the self-giving love of God. It constructs false measures of security, wrongly including those who use them and wrongly excluding those who do not. The God revealed in Jesus Christ shows us a better way.

The Christian testimony to authentic sacramentality is too often construed as a negative one, but it is thoroughly positive. True baptism and communion are absolutely essential for believers. Without them the Christian life of grace through faith and faithfulness by grace is impossible. Outward measures of inward faith simply do not convey this grace, however, nor should one confuse these practices with true baptism and communion.

If we think about how our spiritual lives might become most fully sacramental, three priorities remain. First, acknowledge Jesus Christ as God's saving/revealing self-communication to you personally, and do so often. There is no substitute for responding personally and believingly to God's loving initiative. Second, create the sacramental space in your devotional life to daily feed upon the "bread" Jesus offers through prayer and Scripture reading. There is no substitute for being immersed in the Holy Spirit of Christ. That, and only that, is true baptism. Third, regard the gathered meeting for worship—the incarnate community of people who love Christ and in whose midst he dwells—as the sacramental place to encounter the living presence of God radically. Jesus has promised that wherever two or three are gathered in his name, he will be present in their midst (Matthew 18:20). This is the "real presence" of Christ, and there is no substitute for communing with him in corporate fellowship. That is the essence of sacramental *koinonia*.

While many Christians still employ ritual sacraments, the Quaker testimony on the sacraments is needed desperately by the church and the world beyond it. These are not just sectarian distinctives; they are central insights into the meaning of the gospel revealed by Jesus Christ himself. If we abide in Christ believingly, nothing else is needed. If we do not, nothing else will suffice.

On Spiritual Reality and Its Representations

The testimony of Friends as to the spiritual character of God's working in our lives gets misunderstood in a variety of ways. On one hand, people describe the testimony in negative terms, claiming Quakers do *not* believe in baptism or communion, but this is not the case. Friends *do* believe in authentic baptism and communion as *spiritual* realities, which are accessible to all because of the pivotal work of Christ and the present workings of the Holy Spirit. Believing in God's direct mediating work, Friends emphasize the spiritual character of sacramental realities rather than their formal expressions.

Some religious groups, including some Christian ones, seek to form a priestly bridge between humanity and God, but Christ alone is that bridge. He indeed is *the* High Priest, and anything or anyone attempting to occupy that place actually detracts from his all-sufficient role. Some might even assume that God does not, or cannot, communicate directly with humanity, but the Scriptures and Jesus say otherwise. Indeed, humans fall short in our attempts to attend and ascertain God's presence and direction, but the remedy is to affirm the reality and accessibility of God's active workings rather than resorting to secondhand attempts to represent or effect the real thing. All too easily, the medium becomes the message, and it is Christ alone in whom the world has any hope.

Another misconception is to see the formal disuse of forms as the Quaker approach to sacramentalism. From that perspective, "dry-cleaning" and "fast-feasting" may be set forth as better ways of "getting it done," but this also misses the point. Friends are not arguing for silence or informality as a new and improved form. The primary concern is the inward and authentic celebration of the sacramental life of the gospel—directly mediated through the work of Christ and the workings of the Holy Spirit. Therefore, we seek to create the space to be receptive and responsive to the divine initiative, not to compete with other forms by instituting liturgical informality.

If Jesus indeed came declaring that God is not impressed by formalistic approaches to worship, it is wrong to see Christian religion and forms as the supplanting of Jewish religion and forms; likewise, it is wrong to see Quaker religion as supplanting other forms of Christian religion. The work of Christ does not replace one religion or form with another. Rather, the death and resurrection of Jesus Christ supersede all that is of human origin as the epoch-changing gift of God to the world. It shows that the only way forward for humanity is to receive what God does and has done toward us, and to respond in faith to God's saving/revealing initiative.

A further misconception is that early Quakers opposed the "dead formalism" of their day, and that this applied to other groups but not Friends. Indeed, people who come to worship out of a dull habit or pattern without expecting their lives to be changed are missing out on the central goal of worship: transforming encounter with the living God. This, however, also includes Quaker worshipers. As the first generation of Friends was being followed by a second, a young Friend was awakened from his customary dozing during worship by Anne Wilson, a fiery Quaker preacher. That morning at Brigg Flats Meeting in Northwest England, she challenged him with this trenchant rebuke: "A traditional Quaker! Thou comest to Meeting as thou went from it the last time, and goes from it as thou came to it, but art no better for thy coming; what wilt thou do in the end?"

Young Samuel Bownas indeed was challenged that morning, and having been cut to the quick, he later became a significant leader and traveling preacher among Friends in the early eighteenth century. He traveled to America, and upon returning a couple of decades later, he found himself preaching against the growing complacency that had become a part of an emerging Quaker culture. Critical of spiritual lethargy at home and abroad, Friends have sought to call persons to the vital and transforming reality of the gospel. We preach best when we preach to ourselves.

Friends' opposition of dead formalism, however, does not mean Friends considered "lively formalism" just fine.

Dead formalism was an affront to the everlasting gospel in the middle seventeenth century, but it also is so today, and in every generation. However, even more problematic is the insistence that one cannot encounter the living God unless one does it the right way — religiously. The "right words," religiously-correct postures, orchestrated motions, cultic patterns, manipulated liturgical responses — even by charismatics — these are not what God requires or even desires. While some emphasize the value of their functions, religious prescriptions also can be spiritually unhelpful. Most problematic is that an emphasis upon forms detracts from a focus upon the present spiritual reality. Thus, symbols often eclipse the very relationship they seek to bolster because they are placed between the believer and the object of faith — God.

Forms also can give a false sense of confidence if used, and a false sense of inadequacy if absent. Sometimes out of human insecurity, leaders of worship attempt to elicit a prescribed response from participants, as though such were a measure of spiritual vitality. Or, a group may feel that a particular worship expression is meaningful and may even commend its use if the group would be spiritually alive. It is far better to invite the authentic confession of sin rather than orchestrate "canned" confessions; likewise, more desirable is the spontaneous adoration of God than manipulated words of praise. I imagine God would feel that way, too. These measures fall short of authentic and life-producing worship, and they represent a lack of faith, either in God's ability to touch people directly or in our willingness to respond to God faithfully — or both.

Consider the value of a photograph. When a loved one is absent, a photograph can remind us helpfully of those we love and our relationship with them. I prize photos of my family and loved ones, especially when they are not immediately present. If, however, I am enjoying an intimate dinner with my wife, and while looking into her eyes I place a photo of her between us, gazing at the photo instead of her, my actions might be a hindrance to the relationship rather than a help. Further, they would betray a lack of comprehension regarding the authentic character of intimacy, and I might be asked to move to the garage. Desiring a symbol when the reality is present shows that one has not begun to appreciate the reality itself!

This is how Friends feel when we have cleared aside all else in order to wait in intimate communion with the present Christ, and someone suggests the experience would be enhanced by adding a symbolization of the reality — or worse, "entertaining helps" for the distracted worshiper. Ouch! When this happens, those accustomed to attending the sweet communion availed directly might feel that those uncomfortable with waiting on the Lord miss the essence of sacramentality. This is why open worship is often called "communion after the manner of Friends." Attentive waiting on the Lord reflects a sacramental prizing of directly mediated spiritual encounter with the real presence of Christ in the gathered meeting for worship. As Christ is truly and fully present, he needs not to be represented, but to be embraced, adored, and obeyed.

Friends have opposed both dead and lively formalism in the name of vital and transforming encounter with the present Christ as the new and living way of the gospel. Jesus Christ came not to bring a transaction between God and humanity whereby humans who "do it right" in ways cultic or religious receive God's gift of life. No — the new and living way is the response of faith to God's saving/revealing initiative, and the gospel poses a scandal to all that is of human origin. The good news is that Christ is alive and present, and that those who respond fully in faith to what God has done and is doing receive fully the life-producing gift of God. To this conviction and reality Friends have sought to testify with their words and with their lives.

On Graven Images and Riven Veils

Sometimes the appeal is made that because persons are physical beings, outward sacraments provide a physical help to a meaningful spiritual encounter with God. The ancient Israelites might also have been attracted to the practice of other religions around them which represented their gods with images of stone or wood, but God forbade such "helps" for the children of Israel. For one thing, to worship an image made by human hands becomes a way of worshiping the maker of the idol rather than the Transcendent Being. Idol worship thus becomes self-worship. For another, the object of their worship was not the real God, but a projection of human imagination. Some must have questioned: If the God of the Israelites was the true God, why not invite the making of symbols to represent the living God? With the Israelites, Yahweh established a covenant of faith, whereby God's ways were declared as precepts to be written on hearts of flesh as well as tablets of stone. Therefore, honoring God was expressed as a celebration of God's presence rather than veneration of an image of a distanced God.

As Israel gathered reminders of God's workings in the past, they placed these reminders in the ark of the covenant, imbued with the *shekinah* presence of Yahweh. As they prized the Ten Commandments, Aaron's budding rod, manna, and writings of Moses, they included these items in the ark. Because the power of God's presence was so strong, humans could not survive touching it. Later, when Israel's temple was first built, the ark was placed in the Holy of Holies, where only the high priest was allowed to enter—and only once a year—offering a sacrifice for Israel on the Day of Atonement. While the ark was lost when the Babylonians invaded Jerusalem and sacked the temple in 586 BC, in the second temple period a veil continued to separate the Holy of Holies from the rest of the temple. At the crucifixion, however, the earth shook, and the veil in the Jerusalem temple reportedly was torn in two—riven from top to bottom (Matthew 27:51). As a result, Jesus' followers believed that Christ removed the separation between the holy presence of God and humanity. In the Christ events, God's presence and power become available not only to priests, but to all.

This is a sign of the new covenant, inaugurated by the blood of Jesus Christ. Because of Christ's epoch-changing work, there is no need for a human priesthood, or a physical temple, or animal sacrifices, or the former covenant. Christ has opened a "new and living way" through the curtain by means of his body given for the life of the world (Hebrews 10:20; John 6:51). Because of this world-changing event, all have access by faith now to the *shekinah* presence of God, revealed in the Word made flesh (John 1:14). Therefore, if the full reality of God's saving, revealing presence is available here and now, it need not (and should not) be symbolized. We should simply embrace and encounter it as the heart of the new covenant.

And yet, out of human insecurity or a failure to glimpse the radicality of the new covenant, people are at times tempted to stitch the riven veil back up, creating divisions between people and God, and between one religious group and others. The unmerited and scandalously free gift of God's grace dismays all that is of human origin, which is precisely why a divine revelation is required. No one can come to the Father except being drawn by God (John 6:44-65), not because God requires it, but because humans cannot imagine God's grace on our own. No one has seen God at any time, except the Son. As a result, in an attempt to get it right or to make something happen for people as a transaction with God, well-meaning Christians too often yield to the temptation of religion—seeking to create or further a religious value or experience by something humans do. Consequently, Christian celebrations of communion are often among the most divided religious experiences, even though Christians conduct them in the name of Christian fellowship and unity. A troubling fact, for instance, is that when the ecumenical officers of North America meet for their annual sessions, they come together for all worship services and meetings *except* for the sharing of communion on Sunday mornings. At those meetings, denominational members gather on their own, partaking of the outward elements to the exclusion of even national Christian leaders outside their groups. Generous inclusion of others is often extended, but ironically, the unity-effecting forms do more to mark the divisions between Christian groups than anything else. Here the open and spiritual approach of Friends offers a unitive and non-divisive way forward—and ecumenically so.

When the FWCC (Friends World Committee for Consultation) general secretary and I were asked to lead a brief worship service at the Conference for World Secretaries of Christian Communions in Rome in 2006, a schedule conflict for the person who was to lead the first worship meeting moved the Quaker contribution to the beginning of our sessions. In addition to reading Scripture responsively and playing a Bill Jolliff recording of a song about the wondrous surprises we're likely to discover in heaven, we introduced a time of silent waiting on God as "communion after the manner of Friends." During that time, we invited each one to receive inwardly Christ's gifts of grace, mercy, and empowerment as each needed, doing so with grateful and responsive hearts. We closed the meeting with the shaking of hands, and all seemed to have felt included in the meeting. Interestingly, virtually every one of the half dozen or so worship times after that—led by other leaders of denominations—included a time of sacramental silence before God. Most importantly, Christ was indeed present, and despite differences of doctrine and form between the different groups, we indeed experienced the spiritual oneness we authentically share in Christ.

In celebrating the spirituality of the new covenant through Jesus Christ, Friends affirm with Paul "one Lord, one faith, one baptism" (Ephesians 4:5 NRSV), realities that are spiritual in essence rather than religious, dogmatic, or cultic. To celebrate the sacramental presence of Christ in the gathered meeting, wherever two or three are gathered in the name of Christ (Matthew 18:20), becomes a means of including all believers—even welcoming potential ones to encounter the life-changing experience if they are open. Indeed, the new and living way of Christ calls us to come into God's presence through the new veil, which is the body of Christ. For those tempted to symbolize that reality, the new covenant invites us into something far more transformative: a firsthand encounter with the living God and his world-changing gift of grace.

On Letting Our Lives Preach

If the sacramental principle involves the means by which God's spiritual realities—his love, presence, and truth—are conveyed physically, the Bible has an answer that Friends indeed affirm. When in the fullness of time God spoke to humanity in world-changing ways, he sent a *person*, his son

Jesus Christ—the Word made flesh—in whom the glory of God is encountered and revealed. This involved an incarnational sacramentality, and if that is how God worked in the Christ events, perhaps that is also how God is at work in the here and now. After all, the dynamic lives of persons have greater capacity to convey God's messages to the world than do inanimate objects or symbols, so the changed and changing life of the believer has greater sacramental potency than inanimate forms or objects. Because God works here and now through persons, as his hands and feet in the world, the sacramental question is whether we are willing to become sacramental extensions of God's redemptive and revelational workings in the world. It involves letting our lives preach.

George Fox exhorted Friends of his day with these words, and they certainly speak to members of every generation: "And this is the word of the Lord God to you all, and a charge to you all in the presence of the living God: be patterns, be examples in all countries, places, islands, nations, wherever you come, that your carriage and life may preach among all sorts of people, and to them; then you will come to walk cheerfully over the world, answering that of God in every one." As I think about the meaning of this passage, the incarnational and sacramental question is this: How well are we doing as followers of Jesus in living into the baptism of Jesus and the drinking of his cup?

Baptism with Fire and the Holy Spirit

When it comes to the baptism of Jesus, the operative question involves how to be baptized with fire and the Holy Spirit. Here, the water baptism of John is completely misunderstood by many well-meaning Christians over the centuries. What John the Baptist was really doing involved not instituting a means of ritual cleansing; he was challenging such within Judaism, calling for the "real thing"—genuine repentance from sin and a washing off of old ways of living in favor of living in ways pleasing to God. He thus challenged moral and religious compromises of leaders and called people to higher ethical standards, making a public statement (washing in non-cultic, natural settings) to declare judgment against practices involving outward means of ritual cleansing while morally unrepentant. So to infer John was setting up a ritual and external requirement of water cleansing completely misunderstands the water baptism of John. Rather than bolstering them, John challenged ritual means of purification—of which the Jewish religion of his day had many. Jesus' followers also were criticized for not performing the "correct" washings of hands and other legalistic approaches to more central Jewish values.

Following John, Jesus took that radical move even further, calling for inward purification by the Holy Spirit and with fire as the essential cleansing. In Jesus' teaching, empowering baptism takes place by being filled with the Holy Spirit, so rivers of living (and purifying) water arise from within, and being immersed in the Holy Spirit, so one abides in the Spirit in the entirety of one's life. Sometimes water and spiritual baptism were associated together in the New Testament era, but sometimes they did not overlap, as was the case in Acts 8 and 18–19. If people had been immersed in water but had not received the Holy Spirit, were they *really* baptized? This question caused early Christians to distinguish outward baptism from inward baptism, always prioritizing the baptism of the Spirit as the "real thing" in believers' lives.

Of course, this creates another problem: How does one recognize baptism in the Holy Spirit and with fire? Is it manifested in particular spiritual gifts over others, or by charismatic empowerment over more modest Christian expressions? Here again, Paul poses an incarnational answer. The greatest evidence of whether one is filled with the Spirit is not a particular gift or two; rather, it involves demonstrating the *fruit* of the Spirit: "love, joy, peace, patience, kindness, generosity, faithfulness, gentleness, and self-control" (Galatians 5:22-23 NRSV). Against such there can be no objection! So how will Jesus' true followers be recognized? By their religious trappings? No—they will be recognized by their *love* (John 13:35), itself an incarnational measure.

So how do we receive the baptism of Jesus, with fire and the Holy Spirit? By faith. Just as the gift of salvation comes by grace received through faith, so the gift of sanctification comes as a gift of grace, likewise received through faith and lived out, with divine assistance, in faithfulness. Therefore, the place where spiritual baptism occurs may relate less to rivers, pools, sprinklings, or fonts, and more to the daily devotional practice of receiving the spiritual empowerment of God's grace and availing oneself again and again to the transformative work of God's Spirit in our lives. Like the manna in the wilderness, requiring a daily gathering lest it spoil or become stale, so Jesus as the bread of life must be fed upon daily if the carriage and being of our lives are going to effectively "preach" the gospel, walking cheerfully over the world.

Ingesting the Flesh and Blood of Jesus

A pivotal misunderstanding of John 6:53, where Jesus declares that unless one ingests the flesh and blood of Jesus one forfeits eternal life, infers the outward eucharist is required for salvation. Upon this inference, some Christian groups continue to claim that without taking the eucharist, either in their church or at all, eternal life is forfeited. Such a teaching, however, contradicts John 14:6-7, which declares that Jesus himself is the way, the truth, and the life, and that all who come to the Father do so through him. Note, however, John 6:51, just before the often-misunderstood verse 53. The bread Jesus offers is his flesh, given for the life of the world—a reference to the cross. Therefore, the meaning of this text is that without embracing the way of the cross, the believer cannot hope to receive also the promise of the resurrection. As Paul would have put it, unless one is willing to suffer and die with Christ, one cannot hope to be raised with him on the last day.[2] Note also the importance of abiding in Jesus in the larger passage:

> I am the living bread that came down from heaven. Whoever eats of this bread will live forever; and the bread that I will give for the life of the world is my flesh....Very truly, I tell you, unless you eat the flesh of the Son of Man and drink his blood, you have no life in you. Those who eat my flesh and drink my blood have eternal life, and I will raise them up on the last day; for my flesh is true food and my blood is true drink. Those who eat my flesh and drink my blood abide in me, and I in them. (John 6:51, 53-56 NRSV)

While this passage has eucharistic overtones, it does not specify a cultic act but acts of faithful discipleship in the world; "take the eucharist or be damned" was never the authentic meaning of John 6:53 for its original author or his audiences. The reason Jesus' disciples were scandalized is not that they failed to understand this "hard" saying; the problem is that they understood it all too clearly. The way of the cross always challenges human notions of popularity and success, yet the "flesh" profits nothing. The words of Christ alone are life (John 6:63), and his followers are exhorted to seek the life-producing nourishment that following Jesus brings versus pursuing death-producing alternatives (John 6:27). The stark reality of Jesus' call to embrace the cost is narrated a bit later, where "many of his disciples" abandoned him and walked with him no longer (John 6:66 NRSV).

---

2. For a fuller analysis of this text, see Paul N. Anderson, *The Christology of the Fourth Gospel* (third printing, Eugene, OR: Cascade Books, 2010), 194-220.

Just as Jesus had challenged James and John to drink his cup and to be baptized with his baptism, he called his true followers to be willing to suffer with Christ if required by the truth. Mark 10:38-39 does not issue a promise that Jesus' followers will share with him in cultic rites; it is a warning that authentic followers may suffer with him in faithfulness to the point of martyrdom. Whereas false prophets denied that Jesus came in the flesh (1 John 4:1-3; 2 John 1:7 — implying that followers of Jesus need not suffer in dealing with the pressures of living under imperial Rome), the leaders of John's church called for faithfulness, even if it involved suffering in the world. The faithful witness thus testified that water and blood did indeed flow forth from Jesus' side (John 19:34-35), calling for the willingness to suffer with the Lord as companions on the Via Dolorosa. Therefore, an incarnational view of sacramental living involves not only letting our lives preach, but it also implies being willing to suffer with Christ in the world, in solidarity with him and his community of followers, if required by the truth.

Here the meaning of an often misunderstood statement by George Fox also comes into clear and striking focus. Notice that letting our lives "preach" by our "carriage and life" involves not walking cheerfully over the *earth*, detached from it, or as though part of a frequent-flier program. No, Jesus' faithful followers walk "cheerfully over the *world*," walking with willingness to suffer with Christ in a hostile world, as witnesses against all that is contrary to the ways of God. As Martin Luther King Jr. used to teach, undeserved suffering is always redemptive. So it is for true followers of Jesus in every generation and context.

Therefore, the call to sacramental living is ultimately a call to sacrificial living. Our bodies are offered up as living sacrifices to God, not as a part of some cultic rite, but as a daily offering of our lives to God, no matter what the price

(Romans 12:1). To share with Jesus in the fellowship of his death is to participate with him in the promise of the resurrection. That finally is what it means to be immersed with him in his death and to ingest his flesh and blood. Paradoxically, though, such is the only way to be baptized with fire and the Holy Spirit and to be raised up with him on the last day; and, when that happens, our lives will indeed "preach" and walk "cheerfully" over the world.

"I told them I lived in the virtue of that life
and power that took away the occasion of all wars
and I knew from whence all wars did rise, from
the lust, according to James's doctrine." (**George Fox**, 1651)

"We are a people that follow after those things that
make for peace, love and unity; it is our desire
that others' feet may walk in the same, and do deny
and bear our testimony against all strife, and wars,
and contentions that come from the lusts that war in
the members, that war in the soul, which we wait for,
and watch for in all people, and love and desire the
good of all." (The testimony of Friends to King Charles II, 1660)

"There is a spirit which I feel that delights to do no evil,
nor to revenge any wrong, but delights to endure all things,
in hope to enjoy its own in the end. Its hope is to outlive
all wrath and contention, and to weary out all exaltation
and cruelty, or whatever is of a nature contrary to itself.
It sees to the end of all temptations. As it bears no evil in
itself, so it conceives none in thoughts to any other. If it be
betrayed, it bears it, for its ground and spring is the mercies
and forgiveness of God. Its crown is meekness, its life is
everlasting love unfeigned; it takes its kingdom with entreaty
and not with contention, and keeps it by lowliness
of mind. In God alone it can rejoice, though none else
regard it, nor can own its life…I have found it alone,
being forsaken. I have fellowship therein with them
who lived in dens and desolate places in the earth,
who through death obtained this resurrection
and eternal holy life." (**James Nayler**'s last words, 1660)

"A good end cannot sanctify evil means;
nor must we ever do evil,
that good may come of it." (**William Penn**, 1693)

"From whence come wars and fightings
among you? Come they not hence, even of
your lusts that war in your members?" (**James** 4:1 KJV)

Part VI

Blessed Are the Peacemakers

On Peaceable Ends and Peaceable Means

Most Christians are committed to peace, but the question is whether they are willing to follow Jesus in using peaceable means to peaceable ends. All too easily, well-meaning believers deny the teachings and way of their Lord when confronting evil in the world, yet to do so amounts to a denial of Jesus and his teachings. When George Fox was invited to join Cromwell's army as an officer and lead assaults against the king's forces in 1651, he responded: "I told them I lived in the virtue of that life and power that took away the occasion of all wars and I knew from whence all wars did rise, from the lust, according to James's doctrine." The compromise of moral principle would have been advantageous to this young man, but his first loyalty was clearly to the way of Christ.

This was the first time George Fox was sent to prison, and his refusal to fight cost him six more months in jail. But the imprisonment of the soul is far more enslaving than the jailing of the individual. When asked whether he might like to get out of jail hinging upon being willing to be a participant in warfare, the question Fox asked himself is whether he should follow the example of Jesus and the life lived in submission to the way of the Holy Spirit. When you put it that way, considering what it means to be first and foremost a follower of Jesus, one's options narrow. The way becomes clear, even if it bears a cost.

Asking better questions leads to better answers. A troublesome fact about the world Christian movement is that since the fourth century AD, Christians have been divided on matters of war and peace. In fact, in the two World Wars of the twentieth century, more Christians were killed by Christians than the total number of humans that have been killed in all the wars over the rest of human history combined. This is a troubling fact, to say the least! It is also a major contributor, according to some, to the rejection of Christianity by unbelievers; it obscures their seeing the good Christians have also done.

One wonders how much state-sponsored violence has contributed to Europe's becoming largely a post-Christian society. What I do know is that upon discussing Christianity with several people in Britain and Europe, I have heard a number of thoughtful people share something of the same sentiment: "I don't believe I could be a Christian—I don't believe in killing or war." This is extremely ironic, especially in light of Jesus' clear teachings on peaceable means to peaceable ends. Note that conscientious people sometimes reject Christianity because they feel it is not Christ-like enough; put otherwise, "Christians" have not done well enough at following Jesus.

So how did things come to be this way, and of the various approaches to war Christians have adopted, which approach is closest to the way of Jesus? Historically, three basic Christian approaches to matters of violence and nonviolence have included the following:

Just War

When the emperor Constantine became a Christian in 312 AD, he reportedly marched his army through the river and said that now his was a "Christian" army, his soldiers having been thusly baptized. Until that time Christians had pervasively objected to military service on the grounds that fighting was not "lawful" for a follower of Christ. After the Christianization of the empire, though, Christians were conscripted into service, and within a century the just war doctrine was developed to help define when war was "justifiable" as well as when it was not. While many Christians and non-Christians today hold to some form of this position, such was not the way of Jesus. Although just-war criteria may limit some violence, Jesus did not teach his followers to calculate the cost of violence or even its legitimation. He taught us to calculate the cost of following him with total abandon.

Holy War

During the middle ages, people associated the kingdom of Christ with geographical and political measures, despite Jesus' clear teachings on its spiritual character. Thus, imperial Europe was called "Christendom," and when threatened by invading Goths and such challenges as the expanding Islamic movement, popes and monarchs alike rallied the support of their subjects by applying the holy war texts of the Old Testament to their current political situations. As many as nine major Crusades were launched from 1095 to 1272, and numerous parts of Europe are still paying the cost for violent means to peaceable ends. While many Islamic fundamentalists hold to some aspects of a holy-war position, fewer Christians do today. Like just war, holy war is not the way of Jesus. The "war" into which Jesus enlisted his followers is one we can wage effectively with nothing other than spiritual means and love.

Nonviolent Peacemaking

During the Reformation (1517 and following), the authority of the Bible was recovered. This divided Christianity between those who believed the doctrines and institutions of the Roman Catholic Church were authoritative and those who embraced the Scriptures as finally authoritative. During this era and the next two centuries, three groups came to believe that the early Christians were *correct* in their readings of the Bible and following the way of Christ. The Mennonites, the Quakers, and the Brethren all came to the same conclusion during the sixteenth, seventeenth, and eighteenth centuries, respectively: To say *yes* to Jesus is to say *no* to violence of any sort. They advocated only nonviolent means to peaceable ends and thus came to be called the "historic peace churches." A growing number of Christians are rediscovering the biblical basis for this position today, feeling a "new call" to peacemaking. In the 1980s, no fewer than 11 major parts of the Christian movement in America alone produced statements citing their commitment to peace on biblical grounds. This is a *first* in Western history, and a key reason for this unprecedented movement within Christian history is that weapons of mass destruction cannot be fitted into just war limitations of conflict.[1]

Ironically, present-day divisions on the topics of war and peace among Christians tend to revolve around these developments. Of these three positions, however, only one of them embraces as its central concern following the teachings of Jesus: the nonviolent peacemaking position. Nowhere do Jesus or the apostles ever encourage handling neighborly disputes by launching a holy war or by effecting justice with a sword. In directly challenging such approaches, Jesus admonishes his followers to put away the sword and to respond lovingly to ill treatment; this is absolutely astonishing! It raises

---

1. See the analysis in *The Church's Peace Witness*, Marlin E. Miller and Barbara Nelson Gingerich, eds. (Grand Rapids, MI: Eerdmans, 1994).

pressing questions about how to respond to injustice in the world as well as what it means to be a follower of Jesus. While holy war theologies and just war theories give lip service to the Bible, only the nonviolent approach to peacemaking is based on following the direct commands of Jesus. The others may make use of scriptural examples or citations here and there, but ultimately, they are biblically inadequate.

So what does it mean to be a follower of Jesus? Can one really profess to be his follower while ignoring one of his central ethical teachings? If so, which of his other major teachings — or even which of the Ten Commandments — may we simply disregard, or rationalize away? If we take the teaching and example of Jesus seriously, then nonviolent peacemaking cannot be marginalized as just another denominational "distinctive." We must see it as a basic testimony to what it means to be a follower of the Jesus as revealed in Holy Scripture.

Within a consultation of interdenominational leaders, I once heard John Howard Yoder object to the label "Historic Peace Churches" (as a reference to the Mennonites, Quakers, and Brethren) because it implied the converse was the norm. His suggestion was to consider those using peaceful means to peaceful ends "The Faithful Church" and to affix the rest — even if it is the majority for a while — with a more apt title, such as "Historic Violent Christians" or "The Peaceably Lapsed Churches." He may have overstated the concern a bit, but the point was well-made; all members of the consultation understood it, indicated by knowing smiles and nodding heads.

Why is it that those who aspire to follow Jesus centrally on his central ethical teachings should be a minority rather than the majority of Christians? Like the first Christians, the Mennonites, Quakers, and Brethren have asked not, "What is expedient?" or, "When is killing justified?" but, "What does it mean to be a follower of Jesus Christ?" This should be every believer's first concern, not simply the concern of a cluster of minority voices. The gospel calls not only for the conversion of the world, but it also invites the conversion of the church! And indeed, if the latter happens, the likelihood of the former might actually be advanced.

As a Quaker was debating with a Christian officer regarding the merits of participating in the Revolutionary War, the officer finally conceded that he would be happy to follow Jesus regarding peaceable means to peaceable ends if others would lay down their arms and refuse to be a threat. At this point, the Quaker said: "I see that you would be among the last to follow Christ; I hope to be among the first."

If we really take Jesus seriously and radically—his teachings and his example—a commitment to nonviolent action becomes compelling for authentic followers of Jesus across denominations and from various parts of the body of Christ. The bulk of the Christian movement pulled away from a largely pacifist stance since the days of Constantine; perhaps it might swing back to a more faithful stance at some day in the future. Why not start that shift in direction today? Perhaps authentic "friends of Jesus" can help that happen for the whole Christian movement and beyond. The world would be better for it, and the kingdom of God would indeed be advanced.

On Peace Prayers and War Prayers

At our Friends church in Newberg, once a month we include in our worship services a "peace prayer." During this time an invited member of the congregation shares a particular concern about a situation in the world, or reads a text or Scripture passage for considering, or both. He or she then leads us in a prayer for peace around the world. In this, a modest gathering of believers in the Pacific Northwest feels it has a ministry in touching the world. Such concerns also lend themselves to supporting Christian Peacemaker Teams, building houses for people in Mexico, and making gift boxes to send to needy children around the world and gift packs to give to the needy on street corners. As we pray for peace, sometimes God answers those prayers by yoking us to his service in the world, extending the peace and love of his reign in our local communities and beyond. In that sense, prayer also forms our consciences, and that may be one of its greatest impacts.

Loving families and friends also feel the urgency of praying for their loved ones who are fighting for peace in military deployment, and prayers for the protection and success of these are certainly appropriate within communities of faith. There are few places where God's help and redemptive presence are needed more intensely than in war zones, although praying for alternatives to violence might be the most important preemptive work we can do. We also need to be supportive of families whose loved ones are involved in military service or who have sacrificed so much on behalf of noble causes and motivations, leading to suffering and anguish in long-term ways. On this note, pacifists have not always been as empathic and redemptive as they could be, at times diminishing the impact of their overall testimony to God's love and peace.

In a real way, prayers for peace and prayers for protection go hand in hand, although sometimes we fail to be aware of the consequences of prayers answered. Thus, a worthy question, especially in the years following Operation Desert Storm (which one must consider the most successful war in human history in terms of combatant casualties inflicted to those sustained—over 1,000:1) and the second set of Gulf Wars is: Do we really *want* God to answer our prayers for victory? Mark Twain's "The War Prayer" poses this query with troubling lucidity.

Central to Twain's essay was the long war prayer, in which the minister of the local church petitioned the "Father and Protector of our land and flag"—with such passionate pleading and beautiful language, the like of which had never been recalled—to grant swift victory to our troops. At the close of the prayer, however, a mysterious stranger ascended the podium with a message from the Most High. The message was a request for clarification from God as to whether people really wished the prayer to be answered. "If you would be-seech a blessing upon yourself, beware!" he declared, "lest without intent you invoke a curse upon a neighbor at the same time." Thus, the messenger from the throne translated the other side of that prayer for the congregation to consider:

> O Lord our Father, our young patriots, idols of our hearts, go forth to battle—be Thou near them! With them—in spirit—we also go forth from the sweet peace of our beloved firesides to smite the foe. O Lord our God, help us tear their soldiers to bloody shreds with our shells; help us cover their smiling fields with the pale forms of their patriot dead; help us to drown the thunder of the guns with the shrieks of their wounded, writhing in pain; help us to wring the hearts of their unoffending widows with unavailing grief; help us to turn them out roof-less with their little children to wander unfriended the wastes of their desolated land in rags and hun-ger and thirst, sports of the sunflames of summer and the icy winds of winter, broken in spirit, worn with travail, imploring Thee for the refuge of the grave and denied it—for our sakes who adore Thee, Lord, blast their hopes, blight their lives, protract their bitter pilgrimage, make heavy their steps, wa-

ter their way with their tears, stain the white snow with the blood of their wounded feet! We ask it, in the spirit of love, of Him Who is the Source of Love, and Who is the ever-faithful refuge and friend of all that are sore beset and seek His aid with humble and contrite hearts. Amen.

After a pause, the messenger declared, "Ye have prayed it; if ye still desire it speak! The messenger of the Most High waits."

As bothersome as this flipside of the "War Prayer" is, it reminds us that the perspective of either side in battle is only half the picture. Glorious causes and justified onslaughts often obscure the horrific realities of war—even of victory. Any veteran of frontline warfare can attest to that! The very enterprise of warfare is to inflict enough suffering and carnage to force the other side into humbled submission. We may rejoice at the astounding victories of "smart technology" battles and brilliant strategies, but at the same time we must grieve the horrible loss of human life inflicted by *our* weapons as well as those of our adversaries. The query for followers of Jesus is whether noble ends can ever justify violent means. When I was a teenager, I was personally compelled to consider this question.

"How much evil would you be willing to commit in the name of good?" I can still hear that question ringing in my ears as I listened to Professor L. A. King deliver the morning message that eventful Sunday at Canton First Friends Church. I was about to turn eighteen, and while the Vietnam war was coming to a close, I knew I would soon have to register for the draft at the local post office.

As I pondered the implications of that question, my options became strikingly clearer. I was not so much bothered about the prospect of dying for my country, or for any great cause. I was seventeen! Risk was second nature; I was an athlete. What bothered me was the idea of taking—and training to take—the life of another human being. How could I witness to Christ's sacrificial love while at the same time seeking to kill someone for whom Christ died? Impossible. To allow for any harmful or lethal intentionality was to betray the way of my Lord, I felt. The only option left for me was to object to involvement in war as a matter of Christian conscience; so, within a month I registered as such at the local post office.

Back then it was relatively easy to object to war. The Vietnam conflict became an unpopular one as war atrocities became accessible on the evening news; peace protests enjoyed their "golden age" of influence. But following the collapse of the Cold War and with declared wars on terrorism, it becomes more cumbersome to be proper stewards of a peace testimony today. Indeed, the 9-11 attacks evoke concerns for survival and safety within Maslow's hierarchy of needs, making such ethereal commitments to principle and integrity seem irrelevant. When war is popular, advocacy for peace takes a beating.

On the other hand, these may be among the most pressing of times in which a witness for peaceful means to peaceful ends is needed. There is no better time to inform the conscience of a nation than when there is still time to avert future armed engagements. The time to talk and to educate about peace is always present, whether during a conflict or before a conflict emerges. Most instructive is the fact that the ways an individual or nation deals with a present conflict will inevitably plant the seeds for future relationships—either strained or harmonious—within which future conflicts will either be precipitated or averted.

So how do we help form and reform the conscience of the nation? It begins with first being sensitized personally to Christ's will for his would-be followers. Following Jesus can be a real problem. It may not "work" in short-term, pragmatic terms. It might even get us killed! Certainly, it will bring scorn from the world, and perhaps even from other Christians.

Indeed, myths of victory and domination blind us to the realism of its costs—on all sides. Mark Twain concludes his essay saying, "It was believed afterward that the man was a lunatic, because there was no sense in what he said."

However, we do not follow the way of Jesus because we hope it will be beneficial to us or assume it to be popular; we follow it because we believe it is the way of truth. Forming and reforming the conscience of the nation is far different from simply making a staged demonstration or protest. It begins with first being sensitized to Christ's will ourselves. Then, as we pray, it proceeds by asking—and helping others to ask—better questions, from which better answers come.

On the Sovereignty of Nations and the Kingdom of God

When Margaret Fell carried the message from Friends to the new king, Charles II, in 1660, declaring Friends would neither be involved in treason nor be led, as far as they knew, by the eternal Spirit of Christ to engage in war, a new chapter in history was begun. In contrast to the divine right of kings based on a misreading of Romans 13:1-7, Friends were exercising their faith in the way of Christ as led by the Spirit—refusing to go along with policies against their convictions, but also promising not to be disloyal in their dealings with magistrates. In doing so, they drew a distinction between the reign of Christ and worldly governments of monarchs and regents, while also seeking to negotiate differences between the two. After all, the two paragraphs on either side of Romans 13:1-7 call for loving enemies and living peaceably with all, so that one's witness to the peaceable way of Christ might similarly compel others.

The divine right of kings and queens is no longer as prevalent a notion, but nonviolent peace work faces other obstacles. A key underlying cause of war is a false view of the "sovereignty of nations" in contrast to a genuine understanding of the kingdom of God. The sovereignty of nations goes unchallenged as a nearly sacred modern doctrine, but it is a false one. God alone is sovereign, and those who aspire to be followers of Jesus can put no other gods before him. Worse, in the name of such a doctrine atrocities are committed, even by otherwise Christian leaders; the question is *Why?*

To demonstrate the falsity of the sovereignty-of-nations idea, consider what it would be like if our state governments operated the way national governments did. Suppose, for example, that in response to Oregon real estate being bought up by incoming Californians, the Oregon state legislature decided upon a military campaign against California designed to keep the housing market more affordable for the locals. Or imagine the Michigan legislature declaring war on Ohio because Ohioans were taking up more than their fair share of the auto industry's job market.

These scenarios sound absolutely absurd when one thinks about them in terms of state borders (although when it comes to football, of course, all bets are off)! And yet, if the offending groups were international, a national government might not be equally taken aback by such considerations. At least one culprit is a false conception of the sovereignty of the national state. Of course, nations or individuals acting in violence against other nations is also problematic, so the prevention of such is what a sovereignty of nations doctrine aims to avert; maintaining "sovereignty" allows a group or nation to maintain autonomy and resist being imposed upon by others. Followers of Jesus, however, live by a *different* standard!

To put it into further perspective, it has not always been the case that national disputes within Western governments have been settled peaceably. For instance, it wasn't until the 1660s that the British system of government (on which the American system is largely based) allowed for a "loyal opposition" instead of a violent one. Before Cromwell, the only way to effect a change of government was to oppose the current leadership. Any opposition, taken to its extreme expression, would have ended in an attempt to kill the ruler. Thus perceived opponents were jailed, tortured, or executed simply as a precautionary measure.

Someone stood up, however, and said things don't have to be this way. Early Friends and others sought an alternative to the norm, having sought to influence Oliver Cromwell for many years, in bringing a corporate statement to King Charles II, claiming that they believed the Spirit of Christ would never lead them to take up violence against others. They also suffered violence and were persecuted as a result of laws devised to counter their expansion, yet they did not resort to force or retaliation over the next three decades, leading to the establishment of religious toleration in England. This, and other factors, eventually contributed to the emergence of modern democracy and eventually systems of government that incorporate dissent into the standard process. Meanwhile, intramural political violence has become obsolete.

I wonder what it would take for the same shift to occur globally. Currently, nation-states at times behave on the level of gangsters and ruffians, "robbing the bank" if the repayment of debts becomes too onerous, or following up on threats, as though the issuing of ultimatums justifies their being acted upon. Unfortunately, Christians have sometimes retarded the advance of peace, either due to provincial loyalties or the failure to embrace the nonviolent way of Christ wholeheartedly. But the Scriptures teach that the kingdom of God is never identical to human empires, and we need this distinction now, in our postmodern age, as never before. Implications are as follows:

1. All people, not just one's own people, are beloved of God. While many rejoice at the amazing success of American and allied troops in recent conflicts, we still abhor killing done in our names. We detest the killing of innocent civilians, but we also grieve for the killing of military victims and even victimizers. To consider one's enemy through the eyes of Christ rehumanizes the faces of God's beloved children, who happen to be "opponents" during a particular skirmish. Within God's kingdom there is no division of people along national, religious, or any other sort of lines.

2. Responsibility for one's own extends beyond one's clan, region, and state. To be willing to die for a cause is often easier than to stand by passively, allowing others to suffer victimization. Living by principle is easier when it only affects us. However, leaders who would themselves object conscientiously to war find themselves in a quandary when charged with the custody of others. They feel responsible to protect "their own," and they are. However, if one enlarges his or her "own" to embrace all members of the human family, not just one's home group, new possibilities for peace might surface. The Samaritan, after all, is *our* neighbor.

3. Nations have no real sovereignty; only the kingdom of God is eternal. Might does not make right, and capital offenses are not justified if done in the name of the state. There is a higher law, an eternal principle, whereby the deeds of this life will be judged. Institutions? They will

fade away. Governments? They will dissolve in the passing of time. But one kingdom will eternally abide: that City of God, which Saint Augustine describes as having love as its law, truth as its king, and eternity as its measure.

The sovereignty of nations is ultimately an idolatrous notion. It also bears the additional liability of being false. There is one God over all, whose power is coined in terms of truth, love, and peace — not force, power, and domination. These are values we desperately need for a new world order. The kingdom of God advances in small, unattended ways, and every act of faithfulness and love furthers the way of the kingdom. That is the true battle of the ages, and this is the battle into which Jesus calls each of us to enlist. Over the centuries, Christians have been fierce opponents on the battlefield, but if we really took the teachings of Christ to heart, we may make even better peacemakers. Humans are not the enemy; that which is against the way of Christ, whether at home or abroad, is the true adversary — overcome not by evil means, but by good.

The Counterviolent Way of Jesus

Jesus' counterviolent teachings on peace are entirely clear. He calls his followers to love others — including their enemies — to renounce violence and return good for evil, to embrace the way of his kingdom rather than resorting to force, to serve others rather than seeking to dominate them, to put away the sword, to forgive and not to avenge, and to embrace the cross — even if faithfulness exacts a price. In calling for alternatives to violence, Jesus offers a peace that is not of this world, and he blesses the peacemakers of every generation. That being the case, why is it that many Christians fail to obey the clear teachings of Jesus while claiming to be his followers? Several factors may contribute to believers' failure to follow Jesus on matters of nonviolence; the first involves the hijacking of virtue.

The Hijacking of Virtue

Evil cannot stand on its own; it can only be tolerated if it is presented as a "lesser ill" among forced options or rationalized in other ways. Therefore, in order to compel otherwise moral men and women to take up arms and learn to kill other persons, either a supreme good must be threatened or a worse evil contemplated. Indeed, the values of "God, Mom, and Apple Pie" are yoked to the enlistment of young adults to learn lethal skills of combat in order to avert the sacrificing of other deeply-held values. In the name of "realism" many a principle or ideal has been compromised, sometimes in real-life situations, but far more often as a hypothetical ploy. This involves the hijacking of virtue.

While in seminary, I pastored a small Friends church in Indiana. One Sunday morning, one of our young adults shared with me his plans to join the military. When I asked him why he would be willing to go against the testimony of Friends on the matter, he asked what I would do to protect my family and loved ones if the Russians were to invade. If one is unwilling to let family and friends suffer violence passively, should one not also be willing to take up arms to defend other innocent potential victims in other lands? The point is a good one, of course, as protecting family and loved ones is a God-given responsibility for all. However, gazing over the corn-stalks and rolling hills of rural Hoosier-land, it seemed hard to imagine Russian infantry ever visiting this part of Indiana—either strategically or on furlough. Therefore, the hypothetical threat was totally contrived, and such ploys are used around the world to alter the consciences of young men and women everywhere in order to enlist them in forcible service—whether by armed states or by terrorist organizations.

Ironically, many an idealistic serviceman suffers the rest of his life contemplating the harsh realities of war, where even in the best of exchanges one encounters the sort of suffering (sometimes by his own actions) he was seeking to avert. But that's the realism of war and the result of responding to worldly violence with like means. So, realism deserves consideration on all sides of the issue, not just in enlisting the conscientious into military service. Ask any person who has served in the military, and injuries sustained or inflicted within the fog of war become poignant considerations.

When Jesus was tempted in the wilderness, notice the ways the tempter put forth positive and even virtuous values as a means of enticing him to yield to temptation. Here the discerning follower of Christ will remember that there are never only two options. Rather, with prayer and the creative workings of the Holy Spirit, there is always a third way forward—either around negative outcomes or toward prized values. On this matter, total and unreserved dedication to the way of Christ is the only means of averting the hijacking of virtue. Jesus' teaching comes especially clear on another factor of Christian compromise—the myth of domination.

The Myth of Domination

Another reason some find it easy to disregard the teachings of Jesus on nonviolence is that they misunderstand his teachings on loving one's enemies. They perceive his instruction to "not resist" an evildoer as a call to passivity, when actually the

Greek is better rendered "do not counterstrike" an evildoer. Too easily is "pacifism" (a commitment to nonviolent peace-making) misconstrued as "passive-ism" (doormat passivity), when a closer look at Jesus' teachings shows the exact opposite. Obviously, when the wellbeing of family or friends is threatened, to stand by and do nothing is irresponsible. And yet, the admonitions of Matthew 5:38-48 provide not only an alternative to violence, but far more importantly, a means by which to end cycles of violence endemic in ways "the world" operates.

As Walter Wink[2] and others have shown, Jesus' three exhortations pose a creative "third way" as a means of subverting systems of domination. Prevalent in the Mesopotamian and Mediterranean worlds during biblical times was the myth of domination — still in play today. According to Wink, order and prosperity are promised in exchange for loyalty to dominating individuals and groups, presenting adversaries as evil to be destroyed for the powers of good to be victorious. Therefore, the "powers" held individuals and groups under their sway by forcing subjects into a fight-or-flight posture. After the military established its superiority, "fight" ceased to be an option. The Assyrians, the Babylonians, the Hellenists, and during Jesus' day the Romans all sought to subdue their conquered populations as a means of spreading their empires and influence. Given overwhelming force, people accepted "flight" (or submission) as the only viable way to interact with occupying forces. Jesus as a boy probably witnessed or heard about 2,000 Jewish men crucified near Nazareth as a Roman response to the refusal to pay taxes by Judas the Galilean around 6 AD. Therefore, he understood full well the meaning of the cross during his own ministry.

---

2. Walter Wink, *Engaging the Powers: Discernment and Resistance in a World of Domination* (Minneapolis: Fortress Press, 1992).

Within that context, the admonition to turn the other cheek, in response to being stricken on the right cheek, must be understood contextually. According to Wink, being stricken on the right side of the face would have involved a back-handed slap, assuming people used the right hand for public exchange since the culture considered the left hand unclean. The function of a back-handed slap was not to injure, but to intimidate. It bore with it the threat of a forehanded blow — or worse. If the Jewish subject were to respond with force, the Roman soldier would then have been justified in using lethal force in retaliation. Therefore, the function was to force a subject (usually a leading member of society) to cower and submit. That done, the dominators would have free reign to do as they pleased. *That* was their goal. Turning the other cheek, though, poses a third option. To put one's hands behind one's back, stand up straight, and look the soldier in the eye enacts a bold statement: "Is that a threat? Okay, go ahead. Follow through with a forehand; my hands are behind my back, I am unarmed. Is this the way Rome treats its nonthreatening subjects?" Such a move is designed to shine the light of truth hard on oppression and its systems of operation. In doing so, the citizen under occupation seizes the moral high ground, making it a new playing field.

The second example — giving away one's undergarments when asked for one's cloak — likely related to a creditor's attempt to collect a debt. Who would ask for another's outer garment? According to some legal procedures, if a person owed money to a creditor but could not pay, the debtor could be asked to hand over his outer coat as a means of leveraging payment. But without a home, one would sleep in one's cloak for warmth and protection. To give up not only one's coat but one's undergarments, then, would be shocking. And yet, one's nakedness makes a statement about one's indebtedness and also an unfair system of collection. In Jewish society, nakedness was an affront to the beholder, so this type of action put the pressure back on the creditor, challenging the creditor's uses of leverage — even legally — in collecting debts.

The third instruction, involving carrying the load of another an extra mile, we should see according to Wink as an act of unexpected generosity — again, shining the light hard on "urbane" aspects of domination practices. As Rome was not interested in losing honor in its occupation of Palestine, Rome modified its forcible practices by "limiting" its demands upon its subjects to only one mile of required service. After all, if occupied territories were grateful for the "protection and peace" they received from Rome, people should be grateful enough to help the traveling soldier carry his pack, if requested, at least one mile. Imagine, though, a person refusing to put down the pack at the first mile marker. Might the soldier get called on the carpet by his superiors if word got out that subjects were carrying his load for two miles instead of one? Picture the soldier, now, running after the Jewish subject, begging him to put down the pack, lest the soldier get in trouble with his superior officers. After all, who would believe his story if the soldier insisted he had neither bribed nor threatened the commoner to carry his load twice as far?

Seeing Jesus' teachings on loving one's enemies in this light, the transformative impact of love comes through compellingly. Not only does he exhort his followers to pray for those who treat them poorly, and to return love and forgiveness for subjugation and oppression, but he teaches them to respond in creative and loving ways that actually interrupt spiraling cycles of violence. Enemies are not the adversary; force and domination are. Indeed, even those exerting the means of domination in the world are also ensnared in its mechanisms. But Christ overcomes the wiles of this world, and the way of the kingdom signals an end to the powers of sin and death, calling for repentance and partnership with the good news of the gospel.

Therefore, Jesus calls for his followers to work for the redemption and the transformation of the oppressor in addition to posing creative alternatives to violence. In doing so, Jesus' nonviolent approaches to resistance do not seek victory over violent means by exerting greater violence; they seek to put an end to violence itself by holding out for the ever-present possibility of a third way, which shines the light of truth on a situation and creates an unimagined, redemptive way forward.

The Fallacy of Proof-Texting

Of course, the Bible contains many passages seeming to justify violence, and I believe the fact of God's being presented as commanding the elimination of the Canaanites in the Old Testament is the most difficult theological problem in the Bible. If Jesus represents the same God, and if that God is consistent, how can one square the tribal conquest narratives of Joshua and Judges with the loving teachings and example of Jesus? Of course, holy warfare involved several features of "the ban" — no hostages, no spoils or plundering, no sexual activity, no torture; in that sense, it was totally counterconventional in relation to standard warfare practices of the day. (Interestingly, those who might use the conquest narratives as a basis for contemporary warfare find it rather inconvenient to apply all of the standards used by ancient Israel.) It is also important to note that as well as citing successful episodes of holy warfare, the narratives document exceptions resulting from human failures to follow God's commandments fully. Those incidents also explain why pagan inhabitants still occupied the "Promised Land" in later generations. It was not God's fault. The blame lay with humans who did not follow God fully when they had the chance to clear the land. The point, though, is that using the conquest narratives as a basis for military action by Christians in later generations inappropriately stretches the meaning of the text. Such is never a valid practice for "conservative" interpretations of the Bible.

Those looking for exceptions to Jesus' clear teachings and example sometimes also seize upon a few odd New Testament texts, distorting their meaning to get around Jesus' predominant counterviolent teachings. Some, for example, will build upon Jesus' saying that one must hate one's family in following him (Luke 14:26-27), but this is not an incitement to violence against one's loved ones; it challenges even the laudable reasons people might contrive as a means of excusing themselves from the call to leave all behind and to follow Jesus radically. Therefore, Jesus saying he has come not to bring peace but a sword is not an incitement to violence, but a figurative means of declaring that following him will indeed be costly and painful (Matthew 10:34; Matthew 19:29-30; Mark 10:29-30). Following Jesus will always be hard—especially if it involves the willingness to suffer and die *for* his teachings and his counterviolent mission—yet if one is unwilling to embrace the fellowship of the cross one dare not hope for the fellowship of the resurrection. The nourishing bread Jesus offers is his flesh given for the life of the world, on Calvary. Seeking to preserve the flesh profits nothing (John 6:51, 63); authentic discipleship is always costly.

Another passage found only in Luke cites Jesus as saying, "The one who has no sword must sell his cloak and buy one," after which his disciples produce two swords (Luke 22:36-37 NRSV). Jesus' response—"Enough!"—is terribly misconstrued. While some interpreters infer the Greek to mean something like, "That is enough" (as though two swords were enough to overthrow the Romans), it is better rendered, "Enough of that!" That his disciples misunderstood his message is clarified later, when Jesus declares, "No more of this!" after one of his disciples asks if they should strike with a sword (Luke 22:49-51).

Jesus was calling for an alternative to violent opposition to the Roman presence, not inciting his disciples to armed rebellion; this is consistent also with his clear commands in Matthew and John to put away the sword (Matthew 26:52; John 18:11). Likewise, the wise counsel of Jesus—he who lives by the sword will die by the sword (Matthew 26:52)—is not a declaration that Christians should kill weapon-bearers. It is a warning that if even well-meaning people take up the sword in dealing with their concerns, they may likely die in the same manner. Violence begets violence, even among the otherwise virtuous. Averting zealot-myths of the day was Jesus' point here—literally and directly.

Unworldly Peace

We do not follow Jesus because it is practical. It may even cost us a great deal. We follow the way of Christ because it is true. As Jesus said to Pilate: "For this I was born, and for this I came into the world, to testify to the truth. Everyone who belongs to the truth listens to my voice " (John 18:37 NRSV). The origin of Jesus' kingdom is not of this world; therefore, his servants *cannot* fight to protect it. It is not a matter of permission (may not), but a function of reality. One cannot further Jesus' kingdom by violent means. Rather, violence sets it back. Truth never triumphs by force; it always persuades by convincement. Lasting good can never be accomplished though evil means. The character of the means always affects the complexion of the outcome. Human kingdoms and empires can never be equated with the eternal kingdom of God. Neither nations nor institutions are sovereign; only the truth of God will abide at the end of time, and only truthful and righteous means can further it.

This teaching is all the more striking when set against the backdrop of Jewish and Christian relations with the Romans. While John was probably not finalized until the 80s or the 90s of the first century, Christians had already undergone several waves of persecution by the Romans. Most notoriously under Nero in the 50s and 60s, and under Domitian in the 80s and 90s, Christians had been fed to lions, nailed to crosses, and burned alive for their commitment to Christ. Many times they must have been tempted to "defend" themselves, or at least to strike back and maintain some sense of dignity—as did the Jewish Zealots. The rendering of Jesus' teaching here must have been aimed at countering such inclinations, but notice the approach. Rather than presenting a pacifistic legalism, the biblical text portrays Jesus as getting to the very heart of the matter. The origin of Jesus' kingdom—and the locus of his followers' aspirations—is eternal. This is why his true followers do not, and cannot, fight.

Jesus is indeed a king, but his government is one of truth. In John 18 we have a classic confrontation between true authority and power and their false imitations. One would think Rome's authority and that of its representatives would be absolute, but Pilate is portrayed ironically as being held hostage to the whims of the masses. He tries to set Jesus free, but the crowds will not let him. He claims to have authority to release or to crucify Jesus, but he is presented as then begging the crowd to allow him to let Jesus go, to no avail. Pilate is thus portrayed as the impotent potentate. Finally, the very religious leaders who feel they must put Jesus to death, accusing him of blasphemy, reduce themselves to idolatry, chanting "We have no king but Caesar!" (John 19:15 NIV). Nowhere is irony used more powerfully in John than here. Just as the origin of Jesus' kingdom is from above, so is the source of all true authority. Jesus declares to Pilate, "You would have no power over me if it were not given to you from above " (John 19:11 NIV). The real source of all power and authority is neither structural, nor organizational, nor charismatic, nor popular. It is truth, and this is the character of Jesus' government.

Finally, everyone who abides in the truth hears the voice of Jesus. Again, the non-comprehending statement of Pilate — "What is truth?" — alerts the reader to the writer's scandalizing use of irony. Here, Pilate is exposed as failing to "hear" the voice of Jesus, as are the Jewish leaders. The meaning of abiding in the truth is clarified against the sharp relief of its alternatives. Clinging to conventional means of power, yearning for the approval of the populace, putting confidence in human-made religion, lusting for notional certainty — all of these are exposed as bankrupt idolatries that hinder one's ability to attend, and to hear, the living voice of Jesus. Conversely, all who abide in the truth, and who live out of that reality, hear the voice of Jesus and contribute to his kingdom.

Jesus promises peace to his followers, but his peace is not of this world — either in its origin or its character (John 14:27). In the world, followers of Jesus will face tribulation, and those offended by Jesus will also oppose his true followers. However, his peace is with us and within us. His peace is not the cessation of outward strife, but the victory of love and good and forgiveness over hatred and evil and domination. It is a reality neither worldly force nor violence can touch. From the perspective of the cross all threats lose their teeth; the power of the resurrection puts to death the sting of death itself. In Christ there is peace, for he indeed has conquered the world (John 16:33).

Therefore, in calling his followers to a counterviolent existence, Jesus not only demands we do no harm; he gives us the keys to a new way of being that not only overcomes the world but also transforms it. But for that to happen, we need not only the conversion of the world but the conversion of the church! In Jesus' teachings on peace, Jesus poses an ethic for all Christians, not just an idealistic few. If all or most of Jesus' followers would follow his counterviolent way fully, that would indeed make a realistic difference in the world!

Jesus' Teachings on Peace:
An Ethic for All Christians

The Love Command!

- Jesus commands his followers to love God with all of our hearts, souls, minds, and strength; and to love our neighbors as ourselves (Matthew 22:37-40; Mark 12:29-31; Luke 10:27).
- The trademark by which people know Jesus' followers is sacrificial love for others (John 13:34-35).

"Love [Even] Your Enemies!"

- Jesus calls his followers to love even our enemies, and to pray for those who despitefully use us (Matthew 5:43-48).
- Even the Gentiles and tax gatherers can return good for good, or evil for evil; Jesus calls his followers to live by a higher standard.
- This heaps "coals" onto consciences (Romans 12:14-21).

Renounce Vengeance, and Live by a "Third Way."

- Nonviolent generosity creates new possibilities (Matthew 5:38-42).
- When slapped, stand with dignity; turn the other cheek, risking a forehand strike.
- If someone requests your cloak, give also your undergarments, exposing the system.
- Carry a load twice the distance requested as a means of seizing the initiative.

Our Kingdom Is Other!

- Jesus' kingdom is not of this world — if it were, his disciples would fight to defend it — the truth can never be furthered by force (John 18:36-37).
- But we are to seek first the kingdom of heaven and its righteousness, and all we truly need will be given us (Matthew 6:33).

Servanthood, not Domination, Is "Success"!

- Jesus' kingdom turns things upside down: the first will be last, and the last will be first.
- The Gentiles lord it over their subjects, but not so among Jesus' followers.
- The one wishing to be first must be the servant of all (Matthew 18:4; Mark 9:35; Mark 10:42-45; Luke 22:25-25).

"Put Away Thy Sword!"

- Jesus commands his followers to put away their swords (Matthew 26:52-53; Luke 22:49-51; John 18:11).

- Those wishing to live by the sword will also die by it.

- Peaceable ends require peaceable means, lest the ends be compromised by contradictory means.

"Forgive; Do not Avenge!"

- Jesus commands his followers to forgive even the undeserving (Matthew 18:21-35).

- This is the character of God's forgivingness, and it is also the kind of forgiveness Jesus' followers should emulate.

- As we forgive, so are we forgiven.

"Embrace the Cross!"

- Jesus calls for his followers to embrace the cross (Matthew 10:38-39; Mark 8:34-38; John 12:25-26).

- He who wishes to save his life will lose it, but he who is willing to release his life for the sake of Christ and his way will paradoxically find it.

- Following Jesus may not protect one from persecution — it may provoke it (Matthew 5:10-12).

"Blessed Are the Peacemakers!"

- Peacemakers shall be called the children of the Most High (Matthew 5:9).

- To pursue peaceable goals by peaceable means distinguishes the workings of God from the doings of the world (James 3:18 – 4:4).

- Pursuing peace with all is the way of holiness, without which no one will see the Lord (Hebrews 12:14).

"Peace I Give You, Not of This World!"

- Jesus promises his followers that he will bless us with peace — not as the world gives, bolstered by outward symbols of security, but inward peace — that overcomes the world (John 14:25-27).

- Jesus gives us his peace by means of the Holy Spirit; he invites us to believe.

- That is the only way to overcome the world — trust and obey.

Based on Paul N. Anderson, "Jesus and Peace" in *The Church's Peace Witness,* ed. Marlin Miller and Barbara Nelson Gingerich (Grand Rapids, MI: Eerdmans, 1994), 104-130.

Peacemaking at Home and Abroad

Activists often excel at calling for peace abroad, but living peaceably and harmoniously at home may be another matter. In upholding the Christian peace testimony as followers of Jesus, how well do we embody the values we uphold among those around us—in our communities, our families, our churches, our schools, our places of work? Do we deny the way of the peaceable kingdom in the ways we treat others—even in the ways we work for peace or for other worthy causes? If so, the truth of our convictions is diminished by our actions—perhaps even by our attitudes. Following Jesus not only involves dealing peaceably with our enemies, but it begins and continues with living peaceably and lovingly with those around us.

On these and other subjects, Friends have often posed queries: spiritual questions designed to get to the heart of the matter rather than settling for legalistic boundaries. Sometimes the center may be harder to hit, but that's okay. The goal is living in Christlike ways rather than simply following a prescribed regulation. That being the case, an incarnational witness to the peaceable way of Christ is likely well served by considering the following queries:

- Am I willing to love all people—perceived enemies and friends alike—seeing the other as a person beloved of God, for whom Christ died?

- Am I willing to live forgivingly—not easily offended, but releasing "anything against anyone" readily and joyously?

- Am I willing to trust the power of truth rather than employing force, refusing to influence others unduly by means of enticements or intimidations—appealing to conscience rather than resorting to bribes or threats?

- Am I able to live with transparency and consistency—letting my *yes* be yes and my *no* be no—so that my word is good and can be trusted?

- Am I willing to speak directly to others regarding concerns, in patience and good faith, rather than lobbying politically in order to manipulate a desired outcome—even a noble one?

- Am I careful of the reputation of others, seeking to present their concerns and actions in fair and undiminished light—refraining from gossip and deconstructive references to those not present, at their expense and as an embarrassment to the way of Christ?

- Am I timely and prompt in resolving conflicts at hand rather than letting things fester or suffer additional complications due to careless inattention to their resolution?

- Am I readily helpful to identify and resolve problems at hand, refusing to allow persons or groups to be identified as the problem, but drawing all together as co-laborers in service to the truth and its redemptive application?

- Am I able to live peaceably and harmoniously with all individuals and groups, challenging prejudice and dehumanizing tendencies, within society at large and even within my communities of association?

- Do I draw upon the transforming power of the Holy Spirit so that my attitudes, carriage, and being display the fruit of the Spirit (love, joy, peace, patience, kindness, generosity, faithfulness, gentleness, self-control) as the true markers of discipleship?

- Am I willing to embrace the way of the cross in following Jesus authentically, even if obedience to the truth is costly to self and personal vested interests?

- Am I willing to live receptively and responsively to the leadings of the present Christ—submitted to his lordship and attentive to his leadership—for the furtherance of his reign and glory and redemptive work in the world?

These personal queries help the devoted follower of Jesus work for peace at home as well as abroad, and yet once conflict has broken out the work of the peacemaker is already behind the flow of events. In order to actualize the peaceable kingdom of Christ, carrying out his will in his way—on earth as it is in heaven, preemptive measures can indeed be taken. These include peacebuilding, peacemaking, and peacekeeping endeavors.[3]

Peacebuilding measures begin with ensuring justice, transparency, and honesty. Being downtrodden by the tyrannical breeds corrosive grievance. When transactions are carried out in secret, privileging some at the expense of others, trust in the structures of society is lost. When corruption rewards those who are dishonest, penalizing those who play by the rules, lawlessness is fostered, and stable structures of society are forfeited. Therefore, building solid moral infrastructures within society becomes one of the strongest elements in keeping violence from breaking out. The challenge is not simply one of keeping powers in check; the challenge also extends to building a fair and just society, which is of benefit to all.

Peacemaking measures seek to find a way out of conflict, minimizing the spiral of violence because of a resolute commitment to peaceable means to peaceable ends. Peacemaking refuses to identify persons as the "problem"—the problem is

---

3. For a treatment of peace work in an age of terror, see Ron Mock, *Loving Without Giving In: Christian Response to Terrorism and Tyranny* (Telford, PA: Cascadia Publishing House, 2004).

the problem, and all sides of a conflict are drawn onto the same side as problem solvers working together in constructive unity.

Peacekeeping measures involve maintaining openness and transparency, and seeking to draw input in from all sides of issues. When it is clear who makes what decisions and by what processes, and when those standards are respected, stability results. People can therefore trust systems and others, and all can get about their work more efficiently and effectively.

Two millennia ago Jesus declared "Blessed are the peacemakers," and that statement is true—both then and now.

"They were changed men themselves before they went about to change others. Their hearts were rent as well as their garments, and they knew the power and work of God upon them... And as they freely received what they had to say from the Lord, so they freely administered it to others. The bent and stress of their ministry was conversion to God, regeneration and holiness, not schemes of doctrines and verbal creeds or new forms of worship, but a leaving off in religion the superfluous and reducing the ceremonious and formal part, and pressing earnestly the substantial, the necessary and profitable part, as all upon a serious reflection must and do acknowledge." **(William Penn**, 1694)

"That the Spirit of Christ, by which we are guided, is not changeable, so as once to command us from a thing as evil and again to move unto it; and we do certainly know, and so testify to the world, that the spirit of Christ, which leads us into all Truth, will never move us to fight and war against any man with outward weapons, neither for the kingdom of Christ, nor for the kingdoms of this world." (The Testimony of Friends to Charles II, 1660)

"There is a principle which is pure, placed in the human mind, which in different places and ages hath had different names. It is, however, pure and proceeds from God. It is deep and inward, confined to no forms of religion nor excluded from any, where the heart stands in perfect sincerity. In whomsoever this takes root and grows, of what nation soever, they become brethren in the best sense of the expression." **(John Woolman**, 1746)

"I must give witness 'for life' as consistently and as unambiguously as possible. This witness needs to weave its way throughout all human experience, from the womb to the tomb. This means seeking ways to protect the unborn. This means standing against all forms of prejudice which would dehumanize people precious to God. This means working to eliminate poverty and other dehumanizing social conditions. This means witnessing for peace and reconciliation everywhere possible and laboring hard for genuine alternatives to war. This means seeking out creative alternatives to capital punishment. This means rejecting euthanasia and instead working for a more compassionate end of life environment." **(Richard Foster**, 2004)

Part VII

Testifying to the Truth

Testimonies,
Not Distinctives!

All too easily, the convictions Friends have sought to uphold for the rest of the world to consider are called "distinctives." These are not distinctives, however, but Christian testimonies—articulations of direct implications of the gospel of Jesus Christ. Unfortunately, I may have inadvertently contributed to this confusion, simply by using "Quaker Distinctives" as the title of the second essay in the 1982 edition of *Meet the Friends* (Newberg, Oregon: Barclay Press). That essay does not confuse testimonies with distinctives, as it features particular instances in Quaker history where followers of Jesus have sought to be seekers of truth and advocates for the oppressed, always being open to alternatives to the norm. Nonetheless, commitments to nonviolent peacemaking, authentic worship, inclusive ministry, and incarnational sacramentality may evoke distinctive expressions in particular contexts, so distinguishing a timeless conviction from its contextual expressions is key. Seeking to clarify the difference, I have renamed that essay "Quaker Testimonies and Distinctives" in subsequent editions, introducing the issue as follows:

> Early Friends sought to recover the spiritual vitality of the first Christians, and this led them to raise several *testimonies* to what it means to follow Jesus. While testimonies are timeless convictions, they were applied in timely and distinctive ways. This is why Friends' testimonies and distinctives should *not* be confused.
>
> Friends' testimonies include the convictions that worship should be in Spirit and in truth; that ministry should be universal and Spirit-filled; that sacramental reality is inward and directly mediated; that peaceable means to peaceable ends should be prioritized; that plain speech and simple living are normative for all Christians; and that Christ can be trusted to lead his followers directly if they will attend his present leadership.
>
> But testimonies are not mere "options" for Christians to embrace if they care to or discard if they don't. They are upheld as direct implications of Christ-centered living...distinctive applications of these timeless convictions.

The Christian testimonies of Friends are rooted in the experiences and convictions of early Friends, seeking to follow Jesus and the way of Christ above all else. Even the language of *testimony* and *witness* originates in the Bible, where Jesus testifies to what he has seen and heard from the Father; John the Baptist and others testify to Jesus being truly sent from God; Jesus' words and works testify to his divine commission, the Spirit bears witness to believers, reminding them of Jesus' instructions in timely ways; and finally, Jesus' followers serve as his witnesses in the world. The word for "testimony" and "witness" in Greek is *marturia*; authentic followers of Jesus must be his martyr witnesses in the world.

Therefore, it is not surprising that early Friends' use of the word *testimony* developed with several associations:

1. It had to do with their testifying to the truth of Christ as they understood it. Fox and others bore witness to what they understood to be the testimony of Scripture and the way of Jesus—often in contrast to religious conventions of the day.

2. The most important testimony was experiential. If people had not encountered the power of the Holy Spirit in their own lives—personally—they could not testify to its power to transform and change the world.

3. As Friends wrote about their own lives and those of others, they offered a "testimony" to Christ-centered living as a profitable example for others.

4. Friends came together and issued a testimony to King Charles II in 1660, testifying that they were committed to peaceable means to peaceable ends.

5. Barclay, Penn, and others set out to testify to Friendly understandings of what it means to follow Christ faithfully, applying timeless truths in timely ways.

In "The Testimony of William Penn Concerning That Faithful Servant George Fox" (as an introduction to Fox's *Journal*), two aspects of testimony are noteworthy. First, Penn highlights the testimony of Fox's spiritually transformed life, especially his awesome life of prayer. This was "a testimony he knew, and lived nearer to the Lord than other men." Second, Penn points to the pivotal testimony of the gospel: One cannot be redeemed by Christ outwardly unless one is also transformed by Christ inwardly. Put pointedly, "It is impossible to be saved by Christ without us, while we reject his work and power within us." Therefore, encountering Christ spiritually and personally is central to Christian faith and practice, and the other, particular testimonies orbit around this core.

In his testimony or ministry he much laboured to open truth to the people's understandings, and to bottom them upon the principle and principal, Christ Jesus, the light of the world, that by bringing them to something that was of God in themselves, they might the better know and judge of him and themselves.

From there, Penn addresses nine particulars of timely Christian living, challenging conventional practices of his day. These might be grouped more generally as follows:

- Christians should speak truthfully and plainly, rather than resorting to swearing or false flattery.

- Christians should practice peacemaking constructively and nonviolently, rather than resorting to forcible means.

- Christian relationships and marriages ought to further religious commitments, rather than jeopardize them.

- Christian dress and lifestyles should be modest and plain, rather than ostentatious or frivolous.

- Christian observance of special days and events ought to be ordered by conscience, rather than imposed by culture or the state.

- Christian giving should be in support of inspired ministry and in support of the poor and the needy, rather than forced by a state church.

Since Penn's day, Friends have also borne witness to honesty and integrity, equality and respect for all persons, temperance and freedom from addictive substances, respect for life from beginning to end, care for the earth and the environment, the value of community, and many other concerns. In emphasizing peculiarities of Friends, however, the central basis for our testimonies is sometimes lost.[1] Therefore, embracing and reflecting Christ as the center of our faith and practice is essential.

In bearing witness to Christ-centered living, the following convictions have emerged among Friends historically. At the center is a dynamic understanding of Christ's leadership. Not simply a doctrine or a set of propositions, believing in Christ involves receiving grace by faith, and also living faithfully by grace. If Christ is alive, he seeks to lead the church; if Christ seeks to lead the church, believers can know his will; if we can know Christ's will, we should seek it; if we can know it, we should obey it; if we should obey Christ's will, he will empower us through his Spirit to do so. Therefore, faithful Christian living begins and ends with Christ at the center, and this reality lies at the heart of Christian witness in the world.

The Spiritual and Unmediated Reality of the Risen Lord's Power and Presence: The Center of Faithful Practice[2]

At the center of faithful Christian living is the accessibility of God's presence in the world, mediated through Christ with total sufficiency (John 1:9; 1:12; 14:6). As Christ alone is the bridge between God and humanity (Hebrews 4:14-8:13), there is no need for human intermediaries or priestly substitutes. To add anything to Christ is to diminish Christ; Christ is come to teach his people *himself*. The power and presence of Christ are thus available to all who will but open their lives to divine visitation. This is the good news proclaimed by Jesus and the apostles: the kingdom of God is here and now, inviting a re-

---

1. This is why I prefer to draw on the historic Quaker witness rather than "spicy" acronyms by others.

2. The following outline and diagram are presented in greater detail in my essay, "A Dynamic Christocentricity – The Center of Faithful Praxis," *Quaker Religious Thought* #105 (2005), 20-36.

Christ the Dynamic Center
of Christian Faith and Practice[3]

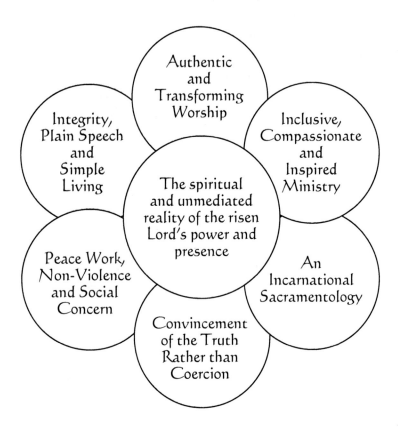

The spiritual and unmediated reality of the risen Lord's power and presence

- Authentic and Transforming Worship
- Integrity, Plain Speech and Simple Living
- Inclusive, Compassionate and Inspired Ministry
- Peace Work, Non-Violence and Social Concern
- An Incarnational Sacramentology
- Convincement of the Truth Rather than Coercion

---

3. Paul Anderson, "A Dynamic Christocentricity — The Center of Faithful Praxis," *Quaker Religious Thought* #105 (2005), 20-36.

sponse of faith to the divine initiative—forsaking all creaturely activity and scaffolding, resting in Christ alone. Implications thus extend to worship, ministry, sacraments, evangelism, peace, social concerns, and personal integrity. Like spokes connected to the hub of a wheel, other convictions stem from the center while also remaining connected to each other as testimonies to the truth of Christ.

Authentic and Transforming Worship

Because Christ is present wherever two or three are gathered in his name (Matthew 18:20), the task is not to invoke his presence; Christ's presence is already a reality. The focus is to open our lives to the workings of Christ, individually and corporately. Therefore, authentic worship is expressive *and* impressive. We express our love for God and receive God's love for us. The goal of worship is openness to the Divine—creating a responsive corporate experience—wherein we attend, discern, and obey the living voice of Christ in the midst. Silence allows us to create the space in which to attend the divine Word—the One Voice beyond the many—but silence itself is not the goal. Likewise, neither is singing and preaching, nor even the making of announcements. God is Spirit and those who worship authentically do so in Spirit and in truth (John 4:24).

Inclusive, Compassionate, and Inspired Ministry

Inspiring worship leads to inspired service, and such is the true measure of gospel ministry, which is inclusive in its scope (including young and old, and women as well as men; Joel 2:28-32), compassionate in its character (written on hearts of flesh rather than tablets of stone; Jeremiah 31:31-34), and inspired in its empowerment (true leaders desire that all God's people were prophets and that God would put his Spirit upon all of them; Numbers 11:29). These convictions in Hebrew

Scripture are fulfilled in the new covenant, and in that sense, the Law and the Prophets are fulfilled in the new and living way of Christ (Hebrews 10:20). Effective ministry involves identifying a need and addressing that need, energized and empowered by the love of Christ — all of which involve a spiritual process and calling.

An Incarnational Sacramentology

As followers of Christ, we must regard sacramental reality (one of the most broadly misunderstood testimonies of Friends), in a positive rather than negative sense. Jesus did not come to replace one religion (Judaism) with another (Christianity) as a form of religious supercessionism. Rather, Jesus challenges all religiosity in calling people to be attentive and responsive directly to God. Indeed, the baptism of Jesus is essential for a vital Christian experience, but it happens with the Holy Spirit and fire rather than by water or human rites (Matthew 3:11). Holy communion is available wherever two or three are gathered in authentic worship (Matthew 18:18-20); to ingest the flesh and blood of Jesus involves embracing the cross (John 6:51-58); and without the cross there is no crown. As an outward evidence of authentic discipleship, the clearest and truest outward sign of an inward spiritual reality is one's changed and changing life. By love for others will the true followers of Jesus be known (John 13:34-35).

Convincement of the Truth Rather than Coercion

Believing we can trust the Holy Spirit to lead us into truth about ourselves (John 16:8-14) means we can trust the Spirit not only personally but also in our witness. As a result, convincement is central to evangelization, which is opposite of proselytization. The truth is always liberating, and it is furthered by testimony, love, and prayer — not by force or coercion. Effective evangelism is a process that involves listening as much as speaking or acting. In dialogue with another, hope fans the flame of the enlightening work of Christ within, leading to a transformative response of faith. Corporately, decision making can and ought to be conducted as a gathered seeking of the will of Christ, which is undivided in its essence. As discernment happens both individually and corporately, effective Christian leadership involves facilitating, attending, discerning, and minding of the present leadings of Christ.

Peace Work, Non-violence, and Social Concern

The way of Christ is central to the means by which we seek to make a difference in the world, and the kingdom of Christ can never be furthered by means counter to its character. Because Jesus' reign is one of truth (John 18:36-37), force cannot further it. Truth liberates, and principle outweighs outcomes; paradoxically, life springs forth from release, and at times unseen possibilities spring forth from the willingness to suffer and even die for the truth. Creative problem solving seeks a "third way." Dichotomies fail to acknowledge the creative work of the Spirit, but the Spirit can always reveal an alternative to the norm. Social concern addresses the particular needs of individuals, but it can also lead to challenging the structures upon which justice is established. In following and furthering the way of Christ in the world, our hope is to actualize the will of God on earth as it is in heaven.

Integrity, Plain Speech, and Simple Living

Abiding in the truth reconciles outward expression with inward conviction. Honesty in business dealings sets the Christian apart from others, or at least it ought to. The Christian's interest in the workplace is in serving others rather than seeking to be served. Integrity of speech means letting one's *yes* be yes and one's *no* be no. Integrity of living involves simplicity of dress and presentation rather than ostentation. Refusal to swear or to use strong language upholds veracity over rhetoric. Seeking to follow the truth is the highest priority — higher than self, group, or cause. As the nineteen-year-old Quaker martyr, James Parnell, wrote to Friends shortly before his death, "Be willing that self shall suffer for Truth, and not the Truth for self."

Therefore, we can see the Christian testimonies of Friends as implications of a dynamic approach to Christ-centered living. As we seek to follow Jesus faithfully we challenge the world and other Christians, as well.

Integrity in Speech and Deed

Striking against the pressure to use disingenuous flattery, Friends committed themselves to plain speech and deeds of integrity. In letting one's *yes* be yes and one's *no* be no, Friends followed literally the counsel of Jesus and James on the matter (Matthew 5:34-37; James 5:12) and encouraged others to do the same. Their faithfulness to Scripture, however, was costly. When appearing before magistrates, Friends refused to swear they were telling the truth, and they suffered imprisonment for doing so. When the government banned meetings held without authorization, Friends still met openly rather than in secret. As a result, entire meetings were imprisoned as authorities sought to disparage dissenting movements.

In 1664, in the city of Reading, England, the local authorities imprisoned all the adults of the Friends Meeting. They came and arrested worshipers every Sunday until all the adults were in prison. Rather than give up, however, and despite beatings and mistreatment, the children of Reading Meeting continued to meet on their own; and they also organized assistance for their parents and friends in prison, providing for their needs. Likewise, Fox and others were frequently punished for not taking off hats before judges and for refusing to use elevated language to address them. Before God, all persons are created equal, and following the example of Jesus, Friends endeavored to treat all persons with deserved respect and dignity.

Plain speech as a timeless testimony, though, may involve distinctive, time-bound expressions. Following the use of the majestic plural *we* by kings of England over several centuries and honoring another individual with the second-person plural *you* (rarely associated with the plural now) became conventions of flattery. Likewise, bowing and scraping and doffing one's hat or referencing another by titles and social status were seen as disingenuous by Friends and others.

Therefore, Friends insisted on referring to others as persons of equal status rather than terms denoting higher (or lower) strata. They used the more intimate terms, *thee* and *thou*, instead of the more elevated term *you*. In present times we might not recognize this language as having the same purpose in regard to differing status associations, so insisting on *thee* and *thou* references makes less sense today. The more general principles of equality and integrity of speech, however, are relevant in every generation, and meaningful applications of such concerns are always welcome.

Plain speech, however, involves more than simply referring to others as equals. It also calls for "speaking the truth in love" (Ephesians 4:15 NRSV), which may involve confrontive words as well as consoling ones. While it is good to want to affirm and edify others, compliments must be genuine. They must emerge from the truth, not calculations of effect. Likewise, we might like to be well thought of, but true and authentic words are worth more than nicely crafted phrases. Therefore, we can welcome critical comments rather than dread them, especially if they are rooted in truth and delivered in love. Friends have thus insisted on the value of speaking and receiving the plain truth out of loving concern for the other. Truth is always a friend and always liberating. Unlike the false prophets of Israel, who tickled the ears of the powerful, the true prophet utters the authentic word of the Lord, and those who receive it are thereby helped.

Of course, discernment and articulation present a challenge. How does one genuinely know what the truth is — about oneself or another — and how does one put a Spirit-led conviction into frail, human language? This challenge has led Friends to commit to modesty of claim, rather than overreaching one's insight. The true word that is right on target needs no embellishment. It can be spoken plainly and humbly. Friends have therefore been reluctant to claim more than is apparent, and willing to describe the perspective from which an observation is made. A story about the Quaker in Yorkshire here applies. When asked if the sheep on the hillside were shorn, he responded, "I cannot say that they are entirely shorn, but it appears that on one side they have been."

Another affront to plain speech is strong language, which plunders highest values in order to make an asserted point. The third of the Ten Commandments forbids taking God's name in vain (Exodus 20:7). Why? Because profanity usurps God's authority — or the power of the sacred — only to step on it as a selfish means of bolstering a claim. Other forms of strong language across cultures desecrate the most intimate and sacred of human relationships and values. That is morally inexcusable. If a thesis cannot be compelling on the basis of its merits, stealing authority from other accounts of value is verbal thievery and not the way of Christ. Christ would have us always speak the truth, and to do so faithfully and plainly. As the apostle says, "But now you must get rid of all such things — anger, wrath, malice, slander and abusive language from your mouth" (Colossians 3:8 NRSV).

And, speaking of truth and love, would we really want others to agree with us if we were wrong? Or agree with us for the wrong reasons? Assenting to a leveraged message affirms coercion, not convincement. Therefore, the goal of discourse is not to entice consent or to win an argument, but to seek and discern the truth. Within that venture, all are potentially constructive partners, and in that sense, all are friends of truth working together as comrades in discernment.

Integrity in word and deed also implies doing as agreed and living up to one's commitments. Therefore, a Friend's word is his or her bond, and one can trust a person who lives with integrity whatever the circumstance. One practical way this conviction took root among early Quaker merchants was that they felt convicted to ask a fair price for their goods rather than resorting to conventional barter systems. They were not the first to use a fixed price system, but in seeking to obey the truth rather than the market, Friends actually became leaders in the marketplace, posting prices clearly so as to alleviate the need for haggling. One could even send a child to buy a loaf of bread from the Quaker merchant. In seeking to do good, Friends did well.

Integrity of speech and deed is the outward expression of living in the truth. Each bit of veiled truth casts a shadow upon the light of Christ, which illumines and liberates the world. There is great freedom in the truth, but the path is one of humility. Genuine humility and self-esteem are always functions of living in the truth, and the root of truth is always the self-giving love of God. As Thomas Kelly says:

> Explore the depths of humility, not with your intellects but with your lives, lived in prayer of humble obedience. And there you will find that humility is not merely a human virtue. For there is a humility that is in God Himself. Be humble as God is humble. For love and humility walk hand in hand, in God as well as in man.

But there is something about deepest humility which makes men bold. For utter obedience is self-forgetful obedience....Out of utter humility and self-forgetfulness comes the thunder of the prophets, "Thus saith the Lord." High station and low are leveled before Him.[4]

Simplicity and Vocation

Simplicity is a factor of prioritization. One cannot do, possess, know, or be concerned with everything; our lives are finite. Sometimes the good we wish to do is threatened by evil or irresponsibility, and if such is the case, the only fitting action is repentance. The fact, though, is that sometimes valid interests threaten our most important ones. Sometimes the good is the enemy of the best. Distinguishing that to which we are truly called from other concerns involves prioritization, and this leads to the simplification of life. Jesus invites his followers to pick up their crosses and to follow him (Mark 8:34), and the cost of authentic discipleship is nothing less than all we have and are.

The main goal of simplicity is freedom. While reducing the clutter of our lives and choosing less instead of more are worthy ventures, the main value of simplicity is that it liberates us to invest our time and energies in really important directions rather than being enslaved to mammon and its distractions. The Christian testimony of simplicity also strikes against societal myths promising to elevate one group of consumers over others. Human worth is not derived from possessions or social status; it roots in the love of God, which we are called to embrace and to share liberally with others. Jesus

---

4. Thomas Kelly, *A Testament of Devotion* (HarperOne, 1996), 36-37

invites us to be anxious for nothing. God cares for the flora and the fauna of the world, and he will also care for our real needs. One cannot serve two masters. The freedom of simplicity liberates us to fully serve God (Matthew 6:19-34).

In addition to plain language, Friends have at times made particular applications regarding plain clothing and dress. In a century where colored clothing set the wealthy apart from others, Friends felt moved to dress in grey or black—modest dress rather than calling attention to oneself. Then again, black or grey silk could still cost as much as colored garb, so even signs of modesty can easily become markers of status if such is valued by a group. Therefore, the overall testimonies of simplicity and modesty will have varied applications, leading to other considerations, such as practicality and value. That being the case, plain and simple dress for Friends in later generations will take into account modesty rather than ostentation, function over presentation, and quality over trend. The focus, however, is not upon oneself, but on how one's actions might affect the welfare of others. For instance, giving clothes and other goods to others in need may be personally liberating, but more importantly, it helps one follow the instruction of Jesus to clothe the naked, care for the sick, and visit the imprisoned (Matthew 25:36).

A concern for simplicity also takes into account the larger picture: economic systems, health concerns, creation care, and sustainability, to name a few. As John Woolman put it, "May we look upon our treasures, and the furniture of our houses, and the garments in which we array ourselves, and try whether the seeds of war have nourishment in these our possessions, or not" (*A Plea for the Poor*). Where people suffer in the production of goods, this may curtail the ease with which we use them. Where harmful diets or substances may jeopardize our health, we may feel moved to forgo products or to modify our consumption. Situations in which it is possible to grow healthy foods locally or patronize those who do may influence our market choices. And, as we think of local and global environmental impacts of our consumerism, such considerations may lead persons of conscience to find alternatives to the norm in prioritizing values and commitments.

Central to the simplification of life is the calling—the vocation—of the follower of Jesus. In contrast to the actualizing of self as the goal in life, the goal of the Christian is the pouring out of self in loving service to Christ and the world for which he died. As imitators of the One who emptied himself even unto death on a cross for the life of the world (Philippians 2:1-11), our priorities become reoriented when we give our lives to Christ. No longer is it our wills that we aspire to carry out; it is the furthering of his will that becomes our foremost concern—that to which we are called. But how do we discern a calling or vocation, and how do we distinguish such from ambition? How do we know (and continue to discover) what we should do with our lives?

The answer orbits around living vocationally. Our first calling is to be disciples of Jesus Christ; the next question involves how our occupations and ventures in life might help us be the best disciples possible, furthering Jesus' work in the world. As Dallas Willard said, "Whenever our first concern is to further the kingdom of God, we will never be without divine guidance as to how that is to happen most effectively." Therefore, our vocational question is not a factor of gainful employability or human aspiration; rather, it has to do with opening ourselves to God's callings upon our lives and being willing to be stewards of all we are and have received.

Discerning one's vocation (or vocations, as callings sometimes occupy various chapters within a lifetime of service) often involves several factors.

1. Reflecting upon life-changing experiences or meaningful aspects of one's life offers a sense of purpose. As we become willing to share something of what we have received, therein lie the seeds of vocation.

2. Jesus invites us to "see how the fields are ripe for harvesting" (John 4:35 NRSV). When the world's needs match our deep yearnings, something profound happens in terms of a calling.

3. As we offer God our talents and skills, we must be open also to rigorous preparation for developing our abilities to serve. Any call to serve is also a calling to prepare, and prioritizing one's energies in preparation for service is the only means to becoming liberated to serve effectively and well.

4. Our vocations develop and receive encouragement within community. As we pray, work, and learn with others, affirmations as to what we should do with our lives lead to clarifications of directions, until we hear the Word of the Lord within: "This is the way; walk in it" (Isaiah 30:21 NRSV).

Living vocationally sometimes involves a calling to public ministry. As the apostle Paul said, "Woe is me if I do not preach the gospel" (1 Corinthians 9:16 NKJV). If such is the case, spiritual and personal preparation for ministry becomes the next step. This will require sustained and rigorous paths of learning, but most importantly it requires an inward deepening in the life of the Spirit, out of which all powerful ministry flows. It will also involve surrounding oneself with mentors and partners in prayer, as deep calls unto deep. A calling to ministry may involve a particular context of service, such as that of a pastor, missionary, or teacher, but sometimes even a clear call to a life of public ministry may take different forms and expressions. Still, the tension between simplicity and vocation connects on the issue of priority. When first things are put first in our lives, the rest seems to take care of itself.

Beyond the scope of full-time Christian ministry, however, Friends have understood Christian vocation to also be relevant within the common ventures of life. Therefore, one may feel called to educate, pursue science, practice medicine, engage in business or industry, conduct social work or civic service, or serve in any number of venues, not despite being a follower of Jesus, but precisely because one endeavors to be the best disciple possible. Friends therefore have seen otherwise "secular" occupations as potential venues of Christian service—serving not in religious language or appearances, but ministering redemptively in service to the Lord. Seeing one's work as a Christian calling also yokes one with Christ in the furthering of his work in the world. This may lead to challenging systems and innovating in order to make things better for the workplace and the world; it may even transform adversity into redemptive possibility.

Historically, when excluded from formal academic settings for refusal to commit loyalty to church or state, Friends started trade and business schools and became masters of the industrial arts. When trees and charcoal were exhausted in the iron industry, Friends began using coal and coke, leading to surprising discoveries. In fact, the Industrial Revolution was closely tied to Quaker innovation in the Severn Valley, as the Darbys of Coalbrookdale found ways to improve iron and steel, leading to cast iron and smelting production. Refusal to use iron for canons and armaments during wartimes allowed Friends to use iron in a variety of other ways. Richard Reynolds replaced wooden rails with iron ones, for example, and the harnessing of steam for propulsion allowed Friends to devise early locomotives. The Stockton and Darlington Railway in northeast England—the first passenger railway—was designed by Quaker Edward Pease, and soon Quaker accountants and bankers—Lloyds and Barclays, to name a couple—organized ways to keep track of business assets and transactions.

In technology, Robert Ransome invented the self-sharpening plow and interchangeable parts for farm implements, making repairs and farming easier. In watch making, such Quakers as Thomas Tampion, Daniel Quare, and George Graham were industry leaders of the day, making it possible for schedules to be kept and for businesses to run according to the clock. In medicine, Joseph Lister found ways to sterilize instruments and doctor's hands prior to operations, making hospitals more sterile and safe. John Fothergill and Benjamin Waterhouse (co-founder of the Harvard Medical School) worked to alleviate smallpox in Britain and America. In chemistry, John Dalton developed the particle theory of atomic elements, and William Allen founded what became the Royal Pharmaceutical Society. Joseph Fry specialized in hygienic soaps, and his company eventually moved toward making chocolate and other products.

In food technology, such Quaker chocolatiers as Cadburys, Rowntrees, and Terrys became leaders in making cocoa and other products. In Philadelphia, Charles Hires advanced the production of root beer as an alternative to more addictive substances. Huntley & Palmers was at one time the world's largest biscuit manufacturer known especially for making water biscuits that would keep for a long time without spoiling, and Carr's (McVities) became known for producing nutritious wafers. As leaders also in woolen and linen industries, Quaker business owners not only sought to serve their customers well, but they also took seriously caring for the needs of their workers. A notable example is found at the Bessbrooke linen mill in Ireland, where the Quaker owners not only built a livable community but also provided a chapel for the worship needs of their predominately Catholic workers. George Cadbury built more than 300 middle-class homes for his workers in Bournville, England, helping them achieve a comfortable level of living, providing for their families and fostering a sense of community. Friends therefore led the way in advancing social welfare as conscientious leaders of industry and society.

Out of concern for the less fortunate, Friends have been pioneers in a variety of other directions. In education, Joseph Lancaster organized schools that would educate whoever wanted to learn. As the large number of pupils created a need for more teachers than were available, Lancaster instituted means by which older and more knowledgeable students taught others and both learned well. Quakers in Kenya have founded hundreds of primary schools, educating entire populations. In mental health, William Tuke founded The Retreat, the first care facility for the mentally ill, in 1796. The Friends Hospital in Philadelphia was founded in 1813, and Elizabeth Fry championed prison reform and more humane care for women prisoners and their families. Friends have also been leaders on social concerns, working steadily for the abolition of slavery, championing women's rights, and seeking to counter the abuse and destructive effects of alcohol. In the nineteenth century, Friends also developed Bible societies and Friends founded no fewer than 12 colleges and universities in the United States alone.

One could go on and on numbering Quaker innovations and enterprise, but the central point is that when one simplifies his or her life, clarifies one's priorities, and lives out of a sense of purposeful vocation rather than aimless actualization, one's life is changed and so is the world. John Woolman believed that if people would live within their means and according to standards of "universal righteousness," there would be no need to pressurize the margins of business and the needs of all could be more readily met. In seeking first God's kingdom and its liberating way, not only are one's own needs met, but the needs of others are more likely to be met as followers of Jesus live by a different standard and transformed priorities. With Kierkegaard, "Purity of heart is to will one thing." That's the power of simplicity. When our callings are clarified and our priorities become realigned, the simplification of life liberates us, empowering our lives to preach and our "carriage and being" to impact the world.

Faithful Witness and Social Concern

Jesus boiled down the Ten Commandments into two—love God and love neighbor (Luke 10:27)—and his ministry sets a fitting pattern for his faithful followers to embrace. Notice that in his ministry he extended God's loving presence to those deemed "sinners"—those beyond the pale of societal acceptability—sharing table fellowship with them even before they repented. He also expelled the money changers and merchants from the temple, challenging a transactional approach to receiving God's grace by means of ritual purity. In regard to the woman caught in adultery, Jesus challenged her accusers, declaring: "Nor do I condemn you; go and sin no more" (John 8:11 NKJV). Jesus became a bridge between people and God, deeming them in the light of extended grace, inviting them to accept having been redeemed by the loving embrace of God.

Jesus also met the personal and physical needs of people, healing the sick, silencing inward voices of pestilence, and feeding the hungry. While he calls his followers not to be anxious over material concerns, much of his ministry actually addressed people's needs socially and materially. He even sent his disciples out in twos, instructing them to expand his ministry numerically and geographically. Following the three-hour sermon of George Fox on Firbank Fell in 1652, the

Valiant Sixty also spread out over the land, traveling in twos, seeking to extend the mission and ministry of Jesus as his faithful followers in their day. Friends have thus always seen Christian ministry as being both inward and outward, spiritual and physical. The cross of Jesus Christ is both vertical and horizontal, and we are called to meet at the center of the two.

Therefore, Friends have long combined travelling ministry involving inspirational and evangelistic preaching with social action and concern — the full expression of gospel ministry. As early Friends traveled in public ministry, sometimes they achieved firsthand awareness of social concerns, which led then to addressing structural injustices in society by means of legislation and the mobilization of societal awareness regarding such issues, and also to working to meet those needs directly. When John Woolman visited a Quaker family and a slave served him there, he asked if her service was bound or voluntary. Upon finding she was a bound slave, Woolman simply got up and left, allowing his silent action to speak judgment for itself. Revivalism and social reform always go hand in hand.

When discerning a particular human need, three levels of response tend to present themselves. First, a set of personal issues may be involved. According to Carlos Marroquin, a sociologist Friend in Guatemala, the most significant socio-economic development in Latin America in the last half century is evangelical missions.[5] When he shared that with me several years ago, I was shocked! His explanation, however, made sense. He told me stories of what happened when people — especially men — responded authentically to the gospel. They tended to give up alcohol consumption and other damaging habits, and they became more faithful to their wives and families and more responsible in their jobs. This means they would be more reliable wage-earners and that their families

---

5. His essay was published in the *Evangelical Friend*, July/August, 1994.

would have a chance for social advancement. Valuing the Bible also led to an interest in learning to read — children and adults alike. As an illustration, he pointed to the construction project near where we were standing. The Friends church was building a school, giving those coming to meeting the opportunity to become literate, and providing real occupational hope for future generations. Again, true social reform begins with changing the hearts of individuals one person at a time, and the work of Christ within is central to societal transformation.

A second way to help is to offer assistance personally. As individuals and communities alike band together in addressing pressing human needs, something powerful happens. God provides through the direct sharing of personal energies and resources; and as we give, we find that God indeed answers prayer, sometimes through his hands and feet — namely ours. When I first came to serve at Reedwood Friends Church in Portland more than three decades ago, I was asked to develop a program for lay-counseling training. Here we sought to prepare the leaders of the church to be effective ministers in their own rights and to provide a healing presence to those in need, while also helping them determine when and how to refer someone to more professional care. Another example of offering assistance personally is that Friends churches in Newberg and elsewhere in the Northwest make trips to Mexico during spring break, where they take supplies across the border and help one or more families build a house to live in. For several years now, faculty, students, administrators, and staff at George Fox University take a full day the second week of the fall semester to send 1,500 volunteers into the community to pull weeds, paint houses, and wash people's windows. Upon sending his followers out to serve their communities, Jesus said, "Freely you have received; freely give" (Matthew 10:8 NKJV), and he invites us to do the same.

Some social needs, however, are more systemic in their origin, and sometimes this calls for structural, societal change. While Friends have not been equally effective or consistent on all fronts, they have made momentous contributions in several historic directions. In the abolition of slavery, for instance, Friends played a major role, far beyond their numbers. For the first century or more of the Quaker movement, some Friends owned slaves, and while neither George Fox nor William Penn challenged the institution outright, Fox reminded Friends as early as 1657 that "Blacks and Indian slaves" were equal with all other people before the Lord and should be treated well. He later wrote to Friends in Barbados in 1676, exhorting them to treat their slaves kindly and to set them free along the lines of the Jewish year of Jubilee. William Edmondson, an Irish Friend, condemned slavery the same year. Concerns grew among Friends on both sides of the Atlantic and in 1688 Friends from Germantown issued a protest to their Monthly Meeting against slavery. In 1693 George Keith published a pamphlet rebuking the buying and owning of slaves by Friends, argued on scriptural grounds. In 1696 Philadelphia Yearly Meeting issued a statement against transporting slaves from Africa, and in 1727 London Yearly Meeting pointedly censured the importing of negroes for slavery purposes. While many Friends in the New World set their slaves free, others found it all too easy to justify their arrangement because their estates and businesses depended upon their labor. They would not go unchallenged for long.

One of the more graphic ways of getting Friends' attention happened during the 1737 Philadelphia Yearly Meeting sessions, where Benjamin Lay called all slave holders apostates. To illustrate his point, this short, stooping man strode into the meeting room dressed as a soldier, holding a hollowed out book containing a bladder filled with red pokeberry juice. In a dramatic flourish against the evils of slavery, Lay pulled out a sword and stabbed the book, spattering what appeared to be blood everywhere. More compelling were the ministries of John Woolman and Anthony Benezet. Becoming convicted that writing a bill of sale for a slave—a fellow human being—was wrong, young Woolman refused to do so, and thus began a fervent campaign the rest of his life to abolish the institution of slavery. His essay against the keeping of slaves was published in 1754, and in 1772 he traveled to London Yearly Meeting, testifying against slavery. On the trip over he contracted smallpox, and he died several months later. Benezet, a Philadelphia Quaker, founded the first antislavery society in America, and his writings influenced John Wesley, Granville Sharp, and Thomas Clarkson to call for the abolition of slavery in Britain. They, in turn, influenced Wilberforce—the leading political opponent of slavery in Britain.

By 1761 London Yearly Meeting had banned Friends owning slaves, and any who did own slaves were disowned. In 1783 British Friends and American Friends petitioned Parliament and Congress to abolish the slave trade, though unsuccessfully. In 1789 Quaker printer James Phillips printed copies of an image of slaves stacked side-by-side in a slave boat, which seared the consciences of those who saw it; Clarkson later made use of it in his pamphlets. In Britain and America Quaker leaders formed the backbones of nearly all abolitionist societies, and women as well as men took leadership in the cause. John Greenleaf Whittier's poetry repeatedly challenged its readers, humanizing the slave as "a man and a brother." Or, as Sojourner Truth put it, after adopting a Quaker family as her own upon achieving her freedom from slavery, "Ain't I a woman?" In 1807 Britain abolished the slave trade and abolished slavery as an institution within its colonies in 1833. Ironically, one wonders if the American Civil War, finally ending slavery in America, would have been necessary if the War for Independence had not been waged some four score years earlier. If America were still a colony when Britain freed the slaves in all her territories, might America have avoided the most costly chapter of the nation's history?

On this note, Lincoln's letter to Eliza Gurney and other Friends (September 4, 1864) raises the poignancy of the conflict. Given that Friends were against both war and oppression, they could "only practically oppose oppression by war." Finally, however, Friends and others succeeded in putting an end to slavery as a witness to God's love for every person and the dignity of each. Leading up to the amendment making slavery illegal in America, such Friends as Levi Coffin and Laura Haviland helped runaway slaves escape to freedom in Canada. As leaders in the Underground Railroad, they helped thousands to freedom.

Friends also contributed to women's suffrage, which emerged out of the abolitionist cause. Ironically, it was as women were helping to overthrow slavery that people began to acutely feel injustices toward women. Because women were not allowed to participate in some abolitionist societies, Lucretia Mott founded the Philadelphia Female Antislavery Society in 1933. Invited as a delegate to the London World Anti-Slavery Conference in 1840, however, she was forbidden to speak, as the organizers were wary about women's issues overshadowing slavery concerns. As a result, Mott organized a women's rights convention eight years later, and along with four others, she drew up a statement affirming that "all men *and women* [emphasis mine] are created equal." Other Quaker women, such as Alice Paul, continued to work for women's rights, and in 1920, the Nineteenth Amendment was passed, giving women the right to vote.

Quakers also played important roles in the temperance movement, seeking to curtail the use and abuse of alcohol. While drinking is not explicitly forbidden in Scripture (drunkenness is; see Ephesians 5:18), the many deaths and injuries caused by alcohol, as well as its being a contributor to impaired moral judgment and predatory victimization, have led Christians of conscience to diminish its use and damaging effects. Quakers and other Christians in America and Britain organized anti-drinking societies. By the 1850s, Friends in Britain had formed the Total Abstinence Union, and the Women's Christian Temperance Union became a formidable force in America a quarter century later. While the legal prohibition of alcohol created new problems with criminality, especially Friends of the Revivalist traditions continued to call for abstinence as the best way to ensure temperance. Key to the Friends testimony on alcohol was the apostle Paul's counsel to avoid eating meat offered to idols (1 Corinthians 8–10). For the sake of the "weaker" brother or sister, one should be willing to forfeit some liberties if required by loving concern for the vulnerable. Therefore, Friends, especially in the evangelical traditions, have tended to embrace a drug- and alcohol-free lifestyle not only for one's personal wellbeing, but also for the sake of others who might struggle with drug- and alcohol-related issues, unwittingly or otherwise.

As faithful witnesses in the world, followers of Jesus cannot but address matters of social concern. Much of Jesus' ministry addressed people's physical and social needs, and authentic Christian outreach addresses both spiritual and physical needs. Sometimes Christian witness happens personally, and sometimes it happens corporately. In all cases, though, abiding in the love of Christ thrusts us into the world he loved, and for which he died. William Penn once said, "Let us see what love can do." We not only conduct that inquiry; we *are* that exploration.

On Radical Discipleship: The Centered Life

The word *radical* bears many associations. It may suggest extremism: "He was a *radical* Marxist." It may imply innovation, or even unconventionality: "Now that's a *radical* idea!" It may even suggest revolution: "Those *radicals*...always wanting to change things." The best meaning of the word, however, has to do with its root, which in this case, is precisely that: *root.* The Latin word for "root" is *radix* (hence, a "radish" is a root vegetable), and *radical* pertains to getting at the root of something.

How about discipleship? A disciple is a learner. Discipline helps one learn. Discipleship involves the endeavor of life-changing learning, and Christian discipleship demands one's enrollment as a humble learner in the school of Christ. So, "radical discipleship" involves getting at the root, the heart, of being taught by the Master. It involves becoming an active learner in the school of Christ.

This venture begins with being "reached" by Christ. In the fullness of time, according to the Scriptures, God sent his Son to redeem the world; but this redemptive mission requires a human response—an act of faith. Faith is simply saying *yes* to God's unmerited favor. And of course, *thank you* follows naturally.

Out of this sense of gratitude emerges not just one act of responsiveness, but an entire lifestyle of living an ongoing *yes* toward God. "Not my will, but Thine" becomes the stance of our unceasing prayer. "If it be Thy will..." ceases to be an escape clause, excusing unanswered petitions, and it becomes the melding of the believer's heart to the will of the Master. "Thy kingdom come, Thy will be done on earth as it is in heaven," becomes the yearning of the Christian, whose vocation has shifted from a means of gainful employment to a lifelong calling to further the way of Christ and his government in the world, transforming it into the peaceable kingdom — the new heavens and the new earth — prefigured in the Scriptures.

Many Christians have abandoned such a vision in the name of "realism," but the Master has not. The eyes of God search to and fro across the land, looking for those whose lives will become an ongoing *yes* to God — those who will worship in Spirit and in truth (John 4:21-24). And upon such responsiveness, the chapters of human history hinge. Upon being convinced of the truth, early Friends set out all over the world to bring the everlasting gospel to any who might need to hear it. In the last century or more Friends have taken inspiration from Christian missionary examples such as David Livingston who followed God's calling to be a missionary doctor in Africa and Albert Schweitzer who was led to do the same. The kingdom of God is an unseen reality, and we are called to further it with our words and also our lives.

Radical discipleship implies living by the way of the kingdom and taking the teachings of Jesus seriously. The first will be last, and the last will be first in God's government. And, those who are "blessed" are the meek, the poor, the persecuted, and the pure in heart (Matthew 5:2-12). These inherit true reward and value when the leadership of God is at work. On one hand, rejection by the world may facilitate our dependence upon God. On the other, God often works through paradox, bringing life out of death and exaltation out of diminishment. And yet, this fact must not allow us to excuse the worldly maltreatment of the vulnerable. The way of the kingdom implies partnership with God in addressing all human need; yet it also bears in mind eternal values and considerations as transcending earthly ones.

This brings us to a crucial matter. All too easily, movements of the Spirit and movements seeking to follow Jesus evolve from a dynamic form of responsiveness into a staid form of organization. On some levels, this is helpful. Organizations routinize maintenance tasks and assign responsibilities clearly so that a group of committed persons can accomplish far more together than individually. However, organizers must beware, lest the dynamic character of the movement be sacrificed in exchange for conventional stability. It is highly ironic that Moses, who yearned that all God's people would prophesy and that God's Spirit would be poured out on all of them (Numbers 11:29), became the foundation of Jewish religiosity, both biblically and ceremonially. It is also ironic that the one who cleared the temple and dined with "sinners" to reveal the extension of God's grace to the ritually "impure" should have been the founder of the greatest religious systems of human history. In these and other cases, the dynamic root of a movement is at times overshadowed by its conventional expressions.

But radical discipleship implies not merely learning about or even imitating the experiences of the founder of Christianity; it involves dynamic engagement with—and experiencing relationally—the *founder*. In this way, radical Christianity is unlike religion proper. It assumes Jesus is alive, and that—as stated before—he is alive seeking to lead his flock. This is why we seek to attend to his leadership, desiring to know and follow his will.

This is also why Quakers have been non-creedal in their faith structures. Creedal systems and legal structures of faith determine what is the least that one must believe and do, or what is the maximum allowed in terms of liberty. Anything inside the "fence" is permissible; all else is unacceptable. Certainly, these systems and structures more easily define "heretics" and "transgressors," and the creeds of the church have always had a two-edged thrust: they include the "orthodox" and exclude the "errant." God, however, might not necessarily view things that way, especially as dogmatic definitions evolve over time. Those "beyond the pale" in terms of a religious platform might not necessarily be beyond the will of the Master, as the tragic history of Christian martyrdom too often suggests. Likewise, those inside the "fold" might not necessarily be attentive to a genuine relationship with the Master nor effective in carrying out his will. So how should the faithful church proceed?

Quakers have posed an alternative approach, which actually goes back to Jesus. It involves aiming at the center of the divine will, not just the legal hedge around it. "You have heard it said, but I say unto you..." declares Matthew's Jesus, and he articulates not a new legal code, but the very heart of the Mosaic law. It embraces a vision of Christian perfection, but it is not perfectionistic, taking into consideration both the divine ideal and the fact of human frailty. While none of us has sole access to God's truth, none of us is devoid of that access, nor can any of us be excused from the calling to seek and mind the will of the Lord.

Jesus' confrontation of Jewish legalism too easily becomes distorted into a new form of Christian legalism, though he was actually challenging structures of religiosity in and of themselves, as well as the well-meaning employment of such approaches by insiders. To follow Jesus radically is to incorporate his means of carrying out the divine will dynamically, not just to replace one religious structure with another. On this matter, Quakers have made an invaluable contribution to Christianity and the world beyond.

Rather than focusing on Christian creeds and dogmatic boundaries, Friends have posed queries to get to the heart of a matter. And, while Friends do embrace doctrines, Friends have also issued "advices"—aspects of spiritual counsel designed to bring the wisdom of the ages to bear on matters of faith, ethics, and morality. The advantage of such approaches is that they appeal to our highest common purposes, not simply our lowest common denominators.

Queries get at the heart of Christian faith and practice.

> Are you careful of the reputation of others?
>
> Do you do all you can to make your homes places in which all who dwell therein are nurtured in the love of God?
>
> Do you conduct your affairs with integrity, and do you fulfill your commitments faithfully?
>
> Do you flee lust and abstain from vanities, keeping your hearts and bodies pure as temples of the Holy Spirit?
>
> Do you so prioritize a life of prayer and devotion that your Christian walk might witness to a transformed life in which the presence of Christ dwells?

Not bad as probing questions to consider! When we aim at the center instead of being content with residing within the boundaries, we may "fail" a bit more as the standard is much higher. On the other hand, by aiming at the heart of the law and attending the center of the divine will, we may more likely succeed at the real thing: attending and minding the Master.

Likewise, advices provide helpful instruction and accountability, but they do so without having to marginalize or punish infractors. They also explain why something is a problem or why particular counsel is advisable, and they make allowance for the inductive seeking out of the Lord's will together. These can lead to meetings for prayer and searching over a particular concern, or even "meetings for clearness" regarding an important decision. "Threshing sessions" can also be called as the group seeks to separate the "wheat" from the "chaff" on a particular issue. Overall, though, the priority in all of these approaches is to attend, discern, and mind the dynamic leading of Christ. This happens in community, but it also involves the earnest searching of each individual as an important part of the larger body of Christ.

One more point deserves to be made regarding the heart and soul of discipleship. Having the willingness to do anything and go anywhere, and as well as being committed to seek the Lord's will in community with fellow believers, the disciple must prioritize his or her own life of prayer and study. Imagine a training program where no personal study time or workout is required. Although some might like that idea, one cannot get very far on a steady diet of secondhand information or distanced observation. One must learn by first-hand engagement in order to make any real progress at anything — whether it be sports, music, academics, or discipleship. Being disciples in the school of Christ involves discipline, and this engagement necessitates a plan which prioritizes prayer, reading, and reflection. A daily plan is usually best, though one should vary the diet to suit one's endeavors. No substitute exists for personal engagement with the Master on a disciplined basis. There is no other road to freedom.

My mentor, Elton Trueblood, used to say, "Knowledge about is never the same as intimate acquaintance with." Radical discipleship ultimately hinges upon intimate acquaintance with Jesus. It is a living and dynamic relationship that plays itself out in the everyday schedules and demands of life. It involves home, and family, and workplace, and hobbies, as well as the calling to be a humble learner in the school of

Christ. In fact, it is precisely within these contexts that both schooling and the performance of learning take place. Only in intimate relationship with the risen Christ can we become true followers of Jesus. As Albert Schweitzer declared:

> He comes to us as One unknown, without a name, as of old, by the lake-side, He came to those men who knew him not. He speaks to us the same word: "Follow thou me!" and sets us to the tasks which he has to fulfill for our time. He commands. And those who obey Him, whether they be wise or simple, He will reveal Himself in the toils, the conflicts, the sufferings which they shall pass through in His fellowship and as an ineffable mystery, they shall learn in their own experience Who he is.[6]

---

6. With this paragraph he concludes this famous book, *The Quest of the Historical Jesus*, ed. John Bowman (Minneapolis: Augsburg Fortress, 2000), 487.

Epilogue

Humble Learners in the School of Christ

As followers of Jesus we must begin the journey intentionally, at some point of our lives, to ever be travelers on it. While we receive God's saving grace by faith, discipleship involves an act of the will. This venture, however, is not a sojourn upon which one arrives at the end after a particular distance. In this life we never fully arrive; we are always to some degree in process. Ironically, the more we learn, the more we become aware of how much we do not know and have yet to learn. This wisdom is rooted in the fact that as disciples—even radical ones—we will always be humble learners in the school of Christ.

Jesus invites his disciples: "Come to me, all you that are weary and are carrying heavy burdens, and I will give you rest. Take my yoke upon you, and learn from me; for I am gentle and humble in heart, and you will find rest for your souls. For my yoke is easy, and my burden is light" (Matthew 11:28-30 NRSV). In following Jesus and embracing his yoke, the burdens of life do not get lighter, but we receive a more fitting and effective means by which to bear them. Our yokes chafe, but his yoke fits properly. Paradoxically, the only way to liberation involves a yoke—the yoke of Christ.

In his invitation to "learn from me," Jesus welcomes us into two realities. First, we learn "of" Jesus as we consider what it means to follow him. His teachings, his example, the effect of his ministry upon those around him—reading and meditating on the gospel teachings of Jesus help us know more about him and how to pattern our lives after his. When we focus on Jesus intensively, connections emerge between what he said and did and how we are to address the needs of the world today as his followers.

And yet, a second meaning also emerges as we consider Matthew 11:28-30 a bit more deeply. The Greek can also be rendered "learn from me," not simply learning of or about him but learning from him directly, as revealed through the Holy Spirit. In that sense, as we seek to follow Jesus faithfully, we can also trust him to faithfully lead us in the paths of truth and in the ways we most need. That is the promise that gives rest to our souls. It is not only grace we receive when we believe in him; it is his grace that also empowers us to follow him faithfully.

In the light of that reality, Christ's heart of meekness and humility speak to us deeply. These qualities—reflective of his character—show the way for us to receive his grace and become humble learners in the school of Christ. And, by the way, matriculation in that school is always open.

CPSIA information can be obtained at www.ICGtesting.com
Printed in the USA
LVOW10s0920180714

394845LV00010B/18/P

9 781594 980282